Living
In
The Light

This book is dedicated to my father, who taught me to think, and to my son, whom I have tried to teach to think. All proceeds from this book will be donated to the Institute of Higher Science for research seeking to eradicate death.

ANNE R. STONE

LIVING IN THE LIGHT

Freeing Your Child From The Dark Ages

Foreword by ELLEN JOHNSON

American Atheist Press
Cranford, New Jersey

First edition January, 2000

Published by American Atheist Press
P. O. Box 5733
Parsippany, New Jersey 07054-6733

Printed in the United States of America.
Product #5588

Library of Congress Cataloging-in-Publication Data

Stone, Anne R., date.
    Living in the light : freeing your child from the dark ages / Anne R. Stone; foreword by Ellen Johnson.— 1st ed.
        p. cm.
    Includes bibliographical references.
    ISBN 1-57884-908-x (pbk.)
    1. Atheism. 2. Religious education of children. 3. Child rearing—Religious aspects. I. Title.

BL2777.R4 S76 2000
649'.7—dc21
                                                        99-059339

FOREWORD

When I was growing up in the sixties and seventies there were few, if any, other children like me and my two sisters, who were being reared without religion. Madalyn O'Hair was rearing her two sons without religion, and neither she nor my parents had anyone to turn to for advice. There weren't any books available at that time to advise the Atheist parent.

What does it mean to rear an Atheist child? When I was growing up, it essentially meant avoiding religion – not going to Sunday school or church, and not praying over peas or bedsides. It didn't include the concept of instilling Atheism into a child. Today there are many adult Atheists who are having children, and they don't just want to rear their children without religion; they want to give them an Atheistic environment in which to live, grow, and learn in as well.

As a parent myself, I realize the importance of providing other Atheist parents with helpful information on how to do this. I am delighted that Anne Stone has written a book about her experiences as the mother of her son Craig and is seeking to share her perspective on rearing Atheist children with other Atheist parents, grandparents, and other caregivers of children.

In this book we get her insights on how to maintain and nourish childhood wonder and curiosity about the world – without leading children into mysticism and submission to unseen forces – as well as how to empower children in the midst of a culture saturated with religious fantasy.

In Chapter Four, "Fluffy Is In Kitty Heaven," we learn how not to talk to children about death. "The grossness of death started me thinking about the way that parents go off on grief and mourning and kitty heaven rather than talking about the guts of death. This evasion of the issue makes sense to the child. It is a fear reaction. It is rolling your eyes and lying so that Mom doesn't catch you. That stricken look that suddenly gets tucked away in a teary-eyed, choked-voice lie is transparent. The child is led onto a road away from gore and guts to a fear so great that Mom and Dad can't talk about it. And guess who steps in with the cure for the fear? Every religion that ever infected the earth has a version of heaven, and/or hell, and/or reincarnation."

Anne Stone shows us how to identify the unique and individual needs of children and how to fulfill those needs with Atheism, so children won't be lured into religions that claim the ability to fulfill them. In addition, she talks about "giving children a scientific way to understand their differences and helping to prevent them from falling prey to religious and occult traps that depend on the differences between people to make them fear alienation and the fear that they might be 'broken'."

Our author discusses the traps set by religion to "snare" our youth and explains how we can protect our children. She shows us how to teach them, with real hands-on activities, about the wonderful world of life and reality. She explains how to cope with it, understand it, enjoy and appreciate it, and how to show our children that the world of reality is far more exciting than the fantasy world of religion. "Give your child memories of childhood. This will fill up the gap that religion seeks to fill. It will make your child "holy" (*lit.* "full of health") and the "holiness" of other families will not be so attractive. Children who are exposed to all kinds of stories will not latch on to the story of the Easter Bunny because they are starving for stories. A market with only one booth gets all the business."

Not all readers will agree with some of the unconventional ideas in this book, but the author's foundational concept cannot be denied: rearing children must begin by respecting them for who they are. Even if you are not a parent, you will find this book educational. Learning how to navigate through life's many social situations as an Atheist is a necessary and helpful skill for every one of us.

I am pleased to offer this book from the American Atheist Press. I hope it will help Atheist parents give their children a good, healthy start at a rational life. I hope it will help to avoid the problems so many isolated Atheists have had to overcome through years of struggle – suffering from fear and guilt, and doing it all on their own.

This is a book our generation will rely upon as much as our parents relied on Dr. Spock.

Ellen Johnson, President
American Atheist Press

CONTENTS

Introduction

The Poor in Spirit

I am often asked why attacks on religion fail so miserably. This is actually the right question to ask and has nothing to do with any kind of weakness in the attack.

Most Atheists are logical, skeptical, rational, thorough, and gifted. Yet, there is only a very small part of religion that can fall before an attack of the intellect. Granted, some of the strongest Atheists I knew were "deconverted" by reading material that taught them to begin to question their religion – for example, the writings of the Christians Paul Tillich and St. Thomas Aquinas. Once a deist begins down the road of questioning, there is no returning to faith. But this fact is misleading. Every one of these "deconverts" was an intellectual who was also bright and skeptical outside of religion. Reading Tillich was only a way to turn a natural skepticism from science or math or philosophy to religion.

In my own twisted path through adolescence I turned to religion as a way to answer the big questions of the world such as, Why is there disease? Because I was skeptical and bright I was able to dump religion after religion and philosophy after philosophy until, in five years, I had run the gamut of them all. It was a kind of obsession with me, for, you see, I had attempted suicide several times. I was one of those extremely sensitive children who felt responsible for all that is wrong with the world. I was extremely serious as a child of five when my brother died and I went on to be the child that everyone in school despises, spending most of my grade school in the hall for fighting with the teacher or to make it fair for the other kids to not have to compete with a gifted child.

I felt guilty. I was depressed and angry. I felt helpless. My passions raged back and forth, forcing my middle school

1

teachers to call my parents demanding that I see a psychi-
atrist. So I know, firsthand, that not all of me was content
with the answers. I needed something more than intellect.

I have always envied people who seemed to be able to
operate their lives with just the facts and nothing more
than the facts. I wanted to suppress the violence of my emotions and be cool and disconnected from passion. Yet, again
and again, against reason, I was drawn to religion. If you
are married to someone who lives with just the facts and
you are a person who lives with just the facts and your children are able to live with just the facts, then you may not
face any greater problems than fighting for your children to
be left alone and free to learn.

If you are married to an emotional person who is tormented by guilt and powerful feelings that need expression; if your children burst into tears any time a goldfish
dies or have violent nightmares or want desperately to get
plastered and play chicken with trains at three in the
morning, then you have a different kind of battle to face.

The place that religions start, the commonality of all
religions, is with a feeling. The Latin word *spiritus* literally
means "breath." That is all. The Christians began to
monopolize this word because of a translation of the Old
Testament where the "breath of God was on the waters."
The Holy Spirit became corrupted, with the word "spirit"
being used for anything supernatural. To be inspired is to
be animated, or filled with breath. To inhale. To expire is to
stop breathing or to exhale for the last time. Religion seeks
to take advantage of the feeling that one lacks animation,
drive, or life and gives "God" as a means by which a person
can become inspired.

The most important key in understanding religion is
revealed in the passage "Blessed are the poor in spirit."
Every religion on the planet seeks to empty humans of
their sense of self, so that they may be "poor of spirit," and
empty them of all the things in life which inspire them:
quest for perfection, love of others, self-betterment, quest
for beauty, quest for knowledge, heroism, pleasure, leadership, and quest for peace. Religion then claims that after

these things no longer inspire, the human is ready for its god.

There is nothing intellectual about this. How many times have you stood before a window or lay awake in the dark or sat up in the morning and rubbed your head and felt like it was all for nothing? "What's the use?" When all the passions are spent when the mind will no longer drive the body, there is that empty, hollow feeling. As a teenager, I lived with this feeling day in and day out. I was so aware of the futility of my life that I wanted to get away from this feeling. I needed inspiration.

Since those years, I have learned that I had been cheated. I believed that my choices were the cold world of science where emotion was in the way, or the passion of religion. Just as science rescued knowledge from the long hand of religious tyranny in the Renaissance, I think that inspiration, the spirit, needs to be rescued from the smothering bosom of religion so that our children can be free to feel as well as to think. Skepticism is a weapon against credulity, but what is a weapon against guilt? How many times is a child encouraged to be bright by one parent and wrapped in guilt by the other for feeling the wrong way or being bad or not being considerate? How is it that a brilliant scientist like the Nobel neurophysiologist Sir John Eccles could be such a paragon of faith? How many times have you been stalemated by the argument of a godmonger that religion makes him *feel* good? Not *think* right, but *feel* good.

Religion is evil. It is a fix. It is a virus that replaces the ability to think clearly and the ability to feel genuinely. To protect a child and to fight all the junkies pushing religion at your child it is necessary to address not just the pat answers and dogmatic thought of religion but the emotional fix: the forgiveness of sin, the alleviation of guilt, the joining with the pack, the relief from fear, and the inspired, higher purpose.

My work inspires people. I am not above using mystical imagery to get across a point, but most of the work is very realistic. At my shows (I am also an artist) people walk around with their eyes bright and their mouths open. They come up to me and gush, "your work is so spiritual!" And I say, "yes, it's part of being human." And they say some variation of "do you feel that you are channeling God?" And I look them square in the eye and answer, "this work is *me* and has nothing to do with a god. I do this work because I am in love with being *alive*."

Teach your children how to be intelligent, but don't forget to teach them how to remember how it feels to be *alive*.

Part One: Who Am I?
The Young Child

Chapter One

The Price of Solace

The Jesuits have a well-known saying: "give us the child until the age of five and he is ours forever." Studies show that 50% of a person's ability to trust is learned in the first year. An additional 25% of this ability is learned in the second year. The human brain doubles in size the first year. If children do not crawl for a certain number of months, they will be dyslexic. All allergies can be cured in the first year, but not after. The human immune system is not able to resist disease until the second year. It is now a given that circumcision is felt by infant boys. It is also known that personality becomes fixed before the age of five, as do learning style, phobias, handedness, self-esteem, independence, and cognitive skills such as modeling, time binding, pattern identification, and verbal ability.

The root of religious susceptibility is in that first five years. If you are new to the parenting game, agree on how to raise a baby and toddler and preschooler. If you think that a religious woman can raise your baby and you can teach the older child Atheism, read the first sentence of this chapter again. Over and over. The battle over a child's soul begins now, at conception.

Vulnerability to religion can be traced back to infancy. So many Atheists believe that religion is an intellectual battle and will be baffled by getting into arguments that turn into shouting matches with the religionist smiling smugly and retreating into faith. Atheists cannot win on this ground. They are not fighting *mano a mano* or mind to mind. They are fighting someone who wants to be persecuted. Every single time a godmonger retreats into faith with that smug smile and the "Well, it's just what I believe!" you must undercut him.

Ruthless is to be without ruth. The religionist is curling up in a ball and showing you that he is wounded and his religion has made him whole. He expects you to be ruthful, moved from pity and moved to mother him. The way to fight on this ground is to go back to that baby. Start focusing in on the fact that it is needy. Bring to light the fact that it is hurt and Mommy left her alone in the dark with the prayer "...if I should die before I wake...." Ask the godmonger who hurt him so badly that he feels so empty and alone. Drive in on the horror of being abandoned. Forget intelligence. This person has brought the battle down from the mountain to the fact of being a mammal. A hurt mammal. Bring into the religionist's awareness, into full consciousness, that he is imploring you to pity him. Do him the service of showing him a mirror to his pain.

When the argument retreats into faith, he is telling you of that dark childhood, showing you the track marks, exposing a junkie seeking a fix for abandonment. The proper response is puzzlement. "How can you live being so miserable?" "What has made you so terrified that you need faith to keep you sane?" "Do you like being miserable?" "Is it fun to be abandoned in the dark and be so helpless and alone and then have someone else save you?" "What if no one came when you called out in the night? What if you knew then that hell was waiting and you called for your god to have mercy on you – and no one answered?"

The religionist will either get furious enough at this point to kill you or break down and start weeping or go into the litany against fear. "My god will not abandon me. My god sees my misery and shall take me up into the light. . ." If you want to go further into this stink hole of unhealed wounds, ask what is feared. Acknowledge that your protagonist is a broken doll on a trash heap and that "god" is the little child that it waits for to rescue it and love it. But I warn you, this can be very, very stressful to watch. It's more than pitiful. You have to have a strong stomach to look at someone's wounds. That's why Atheists like to keep to the high ground: so they won't have to puke with pity.

So who was abandoned?

The anthropologist Ashley Montagu did a long investigation with the question in mind of understanding the differences between the cannibal mind and the non-cannibal mind. He noticed an astonishing thing. In the cannibal tribes, babies were handled as little as possible, nursed only after they screamed for a while, nursed by mothers who held them stiffly – only long enough to satisfy their immediate hunger and then they were left alone again. In non-cannibal tribes, babies were never left alone. They nursed on demand and were carried by the mothers until they wanted down on their own. The cannibal tribes were "toughening" the babies.

For a primate baby to be abandoned is death. Doctors are now saying that babies actually learn to breathe from their mothers. SIDs is now thought to be the baby "forgetting" how to breathe. In the first two years of life, children learn whether it is futile to try to communicate needs or whether it is useful. They learn that the world is a good place full of love or that it is a place where love is unreliable and misery is a part of every waking day. They learn to breathe with a regular deep breath or they learn the ragged wail of despair. The fear of abandonment is never outgrown. It is universal. It is one of the great reasons for turning to religion. "My god! Why have you forsaken me?" Jesus cried it. Moses cried it. Mohammed cried it. It is the baby crying out in the dark, alone in its crib for a parent who is trying to "toughen" the child.

One of the best things a parent can do for a child is to show the baby that this fear of being abandoned is a real concern, a threat to life. If the parent can stand to have that baby in the arms for nine months, the child will react to the world with far less fear, trusting that the parent cares enough to keep it alive. This is something that is extremely difficult to do in this day and age. My own son had to teach it to me. From the moment he was born it seemed that he was a monster of greed. My mother had assured me that babies slept quite a bit and I would have time to myself. Craig made sure that my ears broke every time I set him down. Literally. His grandmother had to rip him out of my arms and talk to me about how he was just upset from not being burped when he screamed and screamed as though she was killing him. It broke her heart. When I tried to get him to sleep in his crib, I was up the entire night. When I was ready to throw him out the window, a wise woman told me, "meet the needs of the baby and you won't have to meet the needs of the adult." So I abandoned my ideas of continuing my career and having a life. It was horrible. But it worked.

"Meet the needs of the baby."

When I talk with Atheists, they say to me, "what in blazes does that have to do with religion?"

Listen to prayers. Listen to the hypnotic words of the faiths. "In the name of Allah, the Compassionate, the Merciful. . ." (Compassion: the consciousness of others' distress together with a desire to alleviate it.) (Mercy: patience with those who err.) "Hail, Mary, Mother of God. . ." "O, Great Mother, who gives us succor..." Do prayers sound like appeals to the intelligence of the deity?

In order to give the child the reality of what it is to live in the world where the arms of mother protect the baby from death, the reality must be there. The need will be. The need will be a memory of pain and terror if the mother is sometimes there and sometimes not. Read here that "mother" is any arms that the baby knows and trusts, father, nurse, babysitter.

Religion claims to offer the arms of mother to the abandoned adult. If you think that denial of this need will keep your children clean of this problem, remember that this is not a "we can't eat cholesterol need" but a need like hunger. If you were to tell your child, "oh, that need to eat is foolish" and religion came along with a feast for a starving man, you would not be beaten by irrationality in your child, but by human nature. The Jesuits know this.

It is now understood that bonding with a baby is an intricate experience. Studies show that if proper bonding does not take place in babies, some of it can be undone later by giving the toddler or the preschooler intense physical contact. Sleeping with them. Holding them, even when they fight back. After the age of five, the child and later the adult will have to live with the fact that this need was not met. It is easy for some and very difficult for others. But it is like having a child who suffers from respiratory problems, who will always be vulnerable to bronchitis, pneumonia, and asthma. The child who didn't get enough physical contact will be vulnerable to cults where everyone stands around and hugs in the emotional bloodbath of the Lord.

When a loved one dies or at the death sentence from the doctor, there will be a great desire to reach out for mother. Without a human there, faith can fill the void, or so the pushers tell us. Priests, Rabbis, and Ministers haunt hospitals like ravens – hoping for the carrion of those afraid of the final abandonment: death.

Chapter Two

The Gift of Words

If babies learn that all they have to do is whimper and mother is right there to figure out what that whimper means, they have learned to trust. But toddlers have more complicated needs and have to overcome the intense frustration of vocalizing that they want their shoes untied because they're hurting their big toes – when all they can do is whimper and then scream with rage when Mom can't figure out what the problem is.

This also has a parallel in religious discussions. "I just can't tell you what I mean!" cries the godmonger, obviously frustrated. "It's just there and I know it's there, but I can't articulate it!" Another way in which an Atheist cannot argue with a deist is when the fuzzy realm of the "spirit" refuses to be defined. Godmongers love this one. The New Age movement wallows in the "ineffable essence of the infinite." You can't refute it if it can't be defined.

Nyah, nyah, ny-nah, nah!

Do you see the face of that toddler peeking at you, testing you? Do you see the frustration of that toddler whose face is about to turn purple from holding his breath because you don't know what he's talking about?

Adults play this manipulation game almost all the time. "You should *know* what I mean, I shouldn't have to explain what I mean." The intellectual falls into the trap of trying to figure out what is going on. But the problem is not in what is going on, it is a translation problem. One of the great problems with most religions is that they have this concept called "direct experience." This is when you directly experience the divine and there is no way to articulate it. If you have had the direct experience you can nod along with the deist, both of you sure of the fact that the other is just as tongue-tied as you are.

12

But toddlers don't like being tongue-tied. It's dangerous for them. "There's a snake at the waterhole, but I don't know the word for snake!" translates to "ahh! Water! agghhhooahh!" And Mom thinks the child needs some water.

The religionist who backs off into the defensive cry of "You just don't understand, it's not logical!" is the toddler who has tried and tried and tried to explain to Mommy about the snake, but has no words. He is the toddler (or the adult) who flies into a rage to hurt himself to punish you for his own inability to communicate.

Craig went from needy baby into smashing his face on the floor so that he could get a bloody nose. As many as six times a day he would fly into a rage where his only desire was to pound himself into a bloody pulp. The grandmothers and the aunts were horrified. These quiet, Christian women thought that, if this child were not controlled, he would become a mass murderer. "Leave him alone!" they urged. "He's just manipulating you!" But I failed to see how Craig who was so obviously in pain could be manipulating me. At twenty months, he could only speak ten words. He could understand, but then when he wanted to tell me something, he would open his mouth as if trying to say the words and nothing could come out. I would try to guess and then the body would arch and the head would start flinging against the floor.

I then decided to teach him sign language. He tore into it like a starving animal. The rages vanished overnight. At thirty months he was speaking in complete sentences, but he actually remembers his release through signing. He has never read the story of Helen Keller, but it would be familiar to him.

As a parent, you can help children to understand that language is not just a way for parents to get their desires through. It is a way for children to give the gift of the word to inner experience. By being patient at this stage and asking questions and helping children to hone in on what they need to express, you are giving them confidence to explain the inexplicable. They gain self-esteem because you have granted them humanity. You don't just order them around and tell them what to think. You convey that you understand that they have an internal world and it is as valid as yours. Children learn that you care vitally about what they have to say – enough to teach them sign language if necessary.

Fighting the godmonger on the toddler level is giving the gift of words. When the conversation is at an impasse because the godmonger feels something and cannot explain it, I look off at the horizon with a dreamy look and start talking about how wonderful I feel to be alive. I talk about the way that seeing a sunrise makes me so full of joy that I start to weep. I talk about missing the little hand of my son. "His hands are so big now." I talk about running in the woods as a little girl with my dog who got run over. I talk about the mystery of stars being giant suns and the way that snowflakes are such pure examples of the beauty of nature.

The deist will be flabbergasted that I have an internal life that is full and wonderful and emotional. I've found that when I start talking about the wonder of life that the deists join in as if this is what they wanted to convey. They learned the words of their internal world from religion. Showing them that the words are independent of their god is a way to grant them the humanity of having their own internal life. When you convey joy and awe in your conversation, the religionist cannot work upon the empty, miserable space that can be filled with the "ineffable essence of the infinite." He is also pulled from refusing to define the unreal to the contemplation of the real. Then comes the quiet voice that says humbly, "you're not religious, but you are spiritual...." It usually trails off.

I usually smile out to that horizon and say, "I am so overwhelmed with the fact that I can breathe." I take a deep breath. "I am real," I whisper. I close my eyes and nine times out of ten the godmonger begins to weep.

Chapter Three

Decision Making

Western religions often model themselves after the family tyranny. The root of family tyranny is in the adage, "Father knows best." Children are told what to do, what to eat, what to wear, how to wear it, where to go, what to say – is it any wonder that, as adults, they need someone to make their decisions for them?

When Craig was little, I began to teach him how to choose. Choosing has to begin with decisions that have no consequence. Choosing between going with Mommy or staying in the car is a decision with consequences which may be terrifying for the child and manipulative on the part of the parent. The first decisions I offered Craig were between this food and that and the order in which food is eaten. Very young children are experienced with food by the age of one. Craig had to make decisions about whether to eat his grated cheese first or his grated carrots. Picking food from a plate often went back and forth and back and forth.

His grandmother was horrified. "Don't let him choose!" she admonished. "It takes too long. How can he know what is good for him?"

But Craig got to choose because I refused to believe that he was a robot. "Do you want to go down this aisle in the store or down the other way?" "Do you want to wear your red socks or your blue socks?" "Do you want to read this book or this book?" Little by little, he learned that he was participating in his life. He was not being shepherded, but he was also not suffering with a world that was too large for him to handle.

I am amazed by the refusal of most of the mothers I have met to let their children make decisions. There is also

15

a lack of questions on the part of the mother. The mother tells, the child listens and asks for clarification, but not too much clarification. Many times a mother will sigh and finally yell, "Stop asking why!" Mothers are supposed to know everything.

Thirty years ago, it was a "fact" that children had to be dressed from head to toe all the time in T shirts, shirts, sweaters, and finally the bunny suit. Mothers are still taught by nurses at the hospital the "proper" way to bundle a baby. Mothers worshiped Dr. Spock. It is now being "rediscovered" that overdressing a baby ruins the body's ability to regulate temperature, so that children "learn" to be too cold or too hot. Since I was a mother who liked to experiment, I decided to let Craig make his own decisions about whether to be dressed or not from the first time he kicked off his blanket over and over. Now we joke about his being "arctic boy." He hardly ever is cold even when I've got on five sweaters. His grandmother still browbeats him into wearing all the shirts and coats she thinks he needs.

When mothers need physical guidance for their children they turn to the doctor. Without question, they follow the advice of the pediatrician. They never read about controversies in medicine. They never question the episiotomy or the circumcision or the relationship between SIDS and use of the DPT vaccine. Europe and Canada have banned this vaccine as being too dangerous. I got into a huge fight with an intern who finally admitted he wouldn't give it to his own children. I had to change pediatricians three times to get Craig out of the hospital because I wouldn't agree to have him circumcised.

A warning about circumcision. Three little boys I know were circumcised later. Their mothers, being zealous about germs, forced back the foreskin to clean the glans penis. Most boys do not have flexible foreskins until puberty. Every one of these little boys suffered from the foreskin cutting off circulation in the penis head and had to be rushed to the hospital for a circumcision. Do NOT wash under the foreskin of your little boy. It is worse than jamming some kind of ear cleaning tool into the ear canal and breaking the eardrum. People can live without eardrums. People can live without foreskins, but who wants to pay the price, especially if you're only five?

So, when the question of morals comes up, mothers turn to the church. The children are there to be shepherded. Jesus is the Good Shepherd. "The Lord is my Shepherd, I shall not want. He leadeth me to green pastures..." – and forces you to eat all your vegetables whether you want to or not. The church is mother who gives us solace and the church is father who tells us what to do.

Most mothers give their babies enough love. Almost every mother in America tells her children what to do. Dads tell their children what to do, too. It used to be that if you disobeyed Mom, Dad came home and spanked you. The God of Wrath shall come down upon the people and smite them for making their own decisions.

Again, Atheists look at me with a funny look and wonder how this has anything to do with religion. Their mothers told them what to eat and what to wear and when to go to bed and how to say their prayers and what to ask about and what not to ask about and they survived. Sure, they survived. Did you have to throw a fit just to get your way? Did you have to become an incorrigible rebel as a teen and turn around and smack your father for trying to spank you? Did your mother weep and weep and wonder where she went wrong and why you don't love her and why you are such a bad, bad child? Good. I hope you loved every minute of it. Kids survive Catholic orphanages, too.

Think back on all those fights. If you think it will make your child strong to fight for what she wants, all right, skip ahead. If you don't want your house falling apart with the tears and yelling and sullen silences, think about it.

Children won't starve themselves. Children won't freeze themselves. Children won't stay awake until they're insane. If they wear one red sock and one orange sock to preschool you can tell them they look ridiculous, but it's their decision. They'll value your opinion far more if they know that you value theirs.

17

Craig and his grandmother have a hair and fingernail battle every time he visits her. I don't cut his hair unless he wants me to. It's the same with the fingernails, although I tell him constantly that they make me cringe. Craig is ten now. His school buddies have started doing the "big jeans" look. He thinks it's stupid. He puts up with all the kids teasing him about having "long hair like a girl!" He said that they stopped teasing him about his long fingernails when he said that they doubled as claws.

A busybody teacher in third grade thought he was a victim of neglect because he chose his own clothes. She also wanted him to do what she thought was the right thing for the class, and he told her to back off and leave him alone. She immediately called his father and his father replied, "If Craig doesn't want to do it, it's his decision." She was horrified. She petitioned me to intervene. I said, "Hey, it's Craig's decision. He'll suffer the consequences." And Craig did. Gladly.

Now with this kind of will power built in by the time your child is five, going to school will not be so traumatic for the child. Sure, it will be traumatic for the teacher, who now has to come up with interesting things to do and get creative about negotiating and selling an agenda. Some teachers will come down with the "wrath of God" approach, but it's difficult for them to fight both parents.

Yet, like the medical side of the picture, the parents have to be involved. It takes time, time, time. The great thing about church and school is that you just hand your kid over and they do all the work. They shepherd little Mary and little Johnny and teach them to be good sheep.

Craig's grandmother once said that children are worthless after the age of five because they stop being obedient. I don't think children should have to be obedient at the age of six months, let alone five years. They're humans after all, not robots or sheep. Remember that apple of the knowledge of good and evil? I think it's great that we get to choose for ourselves. Give little Mary the gift of choosing for herself. She'll love you for it.

Chapter Four

"Fluffy is in Kitty Heaven"

We were walking down the road and we came upon a cat who had been run over. Craig looked at it and said, "What happened to the cat, Mommy?" Uh-oh, I thought. Here it comes. The death thing. It flashed through my mind to avoid the issue, but I took a deep breath and decided to play it straight.

"Cat pancake," I said. "The cat got run over. It's now cat pancake."

You'd thought I had made the joke of the century. For several weeks "cat pancake" was a code phrase for peals of uncontrolled laughter. My sister didn't find the joke at all funny. "How could you say that?" she cried. "That could have been his little kitty! You could have traumatized him!"

"What would you have said?" I asked.

"I would have cushioned the blow and told him about kitty heaven. Cat pancake is gross!"

Yes, it is gross. Of course it's gross. That's the point. Death is attractively gross. Only people don't admit it. Little kids haven't yet learned that it isn't polite to take out grandma's teeth and talk about poop and joke about death.

Most young children are into "gross" in a big way. The insides of things fascinate them. They are drawn to squashed worms and dead birds. They don't find it traumatic to be interested in the guts of things. When we would channel surf and hit a channel where an operation was taking place, Craig would scream if I tried to change from the gore of being inside the box. But children are right. Life has its mechanistic side. Where does food go? What is poop? What happens when we sleep? What is death?

What is death? Not *why* is death. Not *when* is death. But *what*. Death is a cat pancake. You can see it right

19

before your eyes. Death is a cat with its mouth filled with mouse guts. Right there in front of you. Death is a bird on the ground that the ants are attacking. Death is a skeleton. Death is a drowned beetle in a wagon.

The grossness of death started me thinking about the way that parents go off on grief and mourning and kitty heaven rather than talking about the guts of death. This evasion of the issue makes sense to the child. It is a fear reaction. It is rolling your eyes and lying so that Mom doesn't catch you. That stricken look that suddenly gets tucked away in a teary-eyed, choked-voice lie is transparent. The child is led onto a road away gore and guts to a fear so great that Mom and Dad can't talk about it. And guess who steps in with the cure for the fear? Every religion that ever infected the earth has a version of heaven, and/or hell, and/or reincarnation.

When people are exposed to a lot of death, they develop a humor about it. Medical students studying anatomy quickly get the jokes around. They joke about how excited they get when a motorcycle victim comes in because the organs are from a young body. The gore of death is the root of earthy humor down there with doo-doo and how many ways can you hurl if you get drunk enough. Young children love this kind of humor. So do many adults. Remember the grave digger scene in "Hamlet"? "Alas, poor Yorick, I knew him well."

Not only should young children be encouraged to laugh about the gore of death and mess around with guts, they should be introduced to how the body works when they are old enough to understand. If they can understand bad guys and good guys you can introduce germ warfare to them. None of this "eat your carrots so you can grow up healthy" crap. What does that mean to a child? Eat your carrots so the good guys in your body are strong enough to fight the bad guys. Now that makes sense to a tot. You can even explain amino acid chains to wide-eyed six-year-olds. They'll announce to their friends that they "need to eat their beans to complete the amino acid chains for cell protection." That sounds neat. Unless they are particularly prim, kids won't talk about being healthy. That's a yawner. Something Mom makes you do.

Children before the age of five aren't much into grieving. They don't quite grasp the time projection aspects of grief. Grief is a cogitated emotion. Children of this age are into reactive emotions: rage, pain, fear, joy, pleasure, excitement, frustration. They don't usually understand the cogitated emotions that are the bane of school-age kids, and often the death of teens – like indignation, anxiety, reluctance, resignation, anticipation, or depression. They may feel them, but more often they suffer from a reaction to them rather than staying in the second-order emotions. Some parents call it "acting out emotions."

But, a warning: children who are naturally sympathetic are going to feel you feeling grief, big time. They'll feel your fear, too. If Fluffy dies and you or your spouse get upset or start dwelling on the "impermanence of life," the temptation is to try to project your feelings onto children and assume that they are also upset over the death of Fluffy. Wrong. They're upset because you're upset. Why aren't you jumping up and down with joy if Fluffy is in Kitty Heaven? And the long explanation starts about the transience of life and how we're all going to die and how we miss the ones we love when they leave us but we'll all be reunited in Heaven. Oh, and what about that other lie – for the really smart kid who wonders why Fluffy isn't in Kitty Hell, since Fluffy was a bad kitty and scratched all the furniture to bits? You know that lie: "Oh, animals and children go to Heaven automatically because they're too innocent and Jesus loves them."

Okay. Right. So now the child has quite a bit to grasp. The child thinks, "There is a Heaven, and a Hell, but there's something about being innocent or guilty. I wrote all over my father's books and he yelled at me for it but I'm not guilty yet. Hmm. Kitty is in Heaven but we're all sad about it. Hmm. Everyone is going to die. My parents aren't kids so they might go to Hell and we won't meet in Heaven. Hmm. Jesus loves Fluffy, but Fluffy died. If Jesus loves me will I die? Hmm."

I think that every mother or father who starts talking about Kitty or Doggie Heaven is taking a baseball bat and threatening to hit the kid over the head with it. Well, worse, because the baseball bat is real. Yet, why is it that everyone wants to protect a child from death?

I think they're dishonest. They want to protect *themselves* from death.

Stick to the facts. Fluffy is dead. Mommy is traumatized because Mommy has the ability to project in time that Fluffy-ness will not happen in the future. Little Tommy is traumatized because Mommy is weeping and Daddy's mouth is set in a grim line. Everyone is avoiding the questions and lying through their teeth.

Let's back up. Tommy says "Mommy why are you crying?"

Mommy: "Fluffy is dead."

Tommy: "What does that mean?"

Mommy shows Tommy Fluffy. Tommy pokes at Fluffy and Fluffy doesn't act like Fluffy.

Tommy: "Fluffy is dead."

Mommy: "When things are broken and we have to throw them away it makes Mommy sad. We can get a new Fluffy, but Mommy will miss the old Fluffy."

Tommy: "So will I, Mommy. But don't be sad. It'll be okay."

Mommy: "Well, come here, Tommy, and help me be sad."

Nice, clean, maybe a little corny, but conversations with preschoolers can be that way. It is a very rare kid that will project, without prompting, that Mommy will die, too. This usually comes up later. Fluffy is dead. Keep Fluffy (or Rover or Goldie) around for your child to poke and prod and maybe take apart if you can stand it. Remember, death is gross.

Chapter Five

Binding Time and Seeing Feelings

Many of the pictures of children presented by religions and the actualities of children are very different. The big contradiction of the Nineties which will extend into the next century is that the children depicted by religions are not violent, but love their parents and all the older little boys and girls along with all the animals, who lie side by side in peace. The New Age movement is almost tyrannical about the suppression of violence. Violence has become the straw man of concerned religious parents everywhere.

In the Seventies, the famous child psychologist, Bruno Bettelheim, published a work talking about his work with severely disturbed children. *The Uses of Enchantment* was the first book-length discussion of the violence in children's literature and why it was important for children to have access to this imagery. Bettelheim claimed that through wish fulfillment and imagination he was able to give children a handle on their own *natural* violent tendencies. The stories would help them by letting them image their feelings so that the feeling were not suppressed but accessed without actually acting out the violence. Pretend violence is also very important, for the consequences of expressing real feelings were often too traumatic, whereas pretending these feelings in play or with toys would give the child a way to deal with the reality of the feelings without the reality of the consequences.

My niece, who was extremely sick as a baby developed an intense fear of doctors that spread over to include any strange males. Many of the military doctors who treated her tied her down in a chair so they could put tubes in her ears. When she started to get Barbiemania she colored all the Ken images in her coloring book black, carefully going

23

over and over, even ripping the paper, tearing out the pages, and shredding the Ken images. If she could have set fire to Ken dolls she would have.

At one point, and in some countries today, what she was doing was witchcraft and a sign that she was possessed by devils. Some New Age or Christian preschool teacher would have been horrified by the sight of this cute little girl doing voodoo to images of men. The rest of us rolled our eyes but thought it was a very creative way for her to work out her hatred of the men who had tied her down and hurt her. Today, she is still a little shy of strange men, but she has a wild crush on the little boy who took her to the Cinderella Ball.

Children are violent. When flower power was in and people said things like "bless the beasts and the children" after the hit song, the children were swinging from trees trying to "kill" each other with pretend guns in complicated war games. The suppression of "violence" games has led to more violent children. One of the advantages of sports is that they allow one to act out "violence." Men who are familiar with sports have a better sense of what happens when they pound someone and how far they can go before they blow up. But much better than sports are bloodthirsty video games or having violent dreams.

Pretend violence is one aspect of what I call "seeing feelings." The signal that a feeling is taboo in a society is the increase of counter culture avenues to explore the forbidden feelings in the realm of the imagination.

We used to have a saying that "if you wanted to meet the worst kid, go see the preacher's kid." Look at modern religious literature aimed at children. The sickeningly sweet smell of it reeks of a funeral. Religious people say that it is reactionary, because of all the violence in children's literature, but children's literature is more or less violent as a reaction of the time in which the child finds himself.

I am afraid for the religious. How many little girls are out there that need to color Ken black, but are not allowed? They carry these repressed feelings until they can take them out on someone. Maybe their hatred is subtle, but maybe it's not and little Mary Good Christian stabs her husband to death one night. I often see mothers who have suppressed "violence" in their families turn their backs and never see their kids kicking and pinching each other with a viciousness that is eerie.

Again, it seems obvious that if small children are having problems that it is important for the parents to try to help them communicate their feelings and understand what it really is that bothers them. Children just aren't evil out of the blue. They don't suffer from possession by demons.

I mistakenly thought that giving Craig a doll would help him learn to be nurturing. "Eddy" the doll got his clothes stripped off and flew over the stairwell to land on his head several times a day. There was no way that doll was going to be cuddled or fed or clothed or put to bed. I thought that if Craig wasn't exposed to TV he wouldn't take up shooting people with sticks and anything else that looked like a gun. I wasn't anti guns, I was just curious. Craig took to designing elaborate traps to kill animals and talked quite a bit about torturing them and digging out their guts.

Part of the problem with reading Bible stories or nice PC non-violent New Ages stories to the exclusion of everything else is that children do not learn to act out their own stories. It may be violent. It may be gory. It may be taboo, but it's a story that a child needs as much as a thousand repetitions of "one, two, tie your shoe." Many religious stories are not only devoid of violence but also devoid of humor of the childish kind – the Bugs Bunny kind. Zany, wild, uncontrolled, and very violent, Bugs shows children (and adults) their wild sides. Children don't usually act like Bugs, but they love Bugs. Bugs is great because he is so irreverent and rarely shows fear. He isn't anxious about the world, but runs when he has to. To me, Bugs is sort of the antipathy of a Bible story. Bugs shows us why it is important to laugh at the Daffys and the Elmers of the world. Can you imagine Bugs being PC?

Part of a way to help children fit in later in school, is to let them go wild with their imaginations now. There is a story that Jane Goodall tells of a chimp named Mike who was crippled. Mike discovered that he could get the attention of the group of apes by banging on garbage lids. Soon, he and his brother were the alpha apes despite his obvious handicap. If your child has wild tales of wacky, violent, goofy, gory, out-there stuff, other kids won't be able to resist wanting to be friends. Craig, an introverted child who despised Santa was mobbed in school when he finally went. I asked one of the kids why Craig was so popular.

"Because he always thinks of such interesting things to do!" the kid exclaimed.

The other important skill that young children learn is binding time with stories. First this happens, then this happens, then the end. All stories help children learn to create a narrative in their minds. It is very important for children not only to listen to stories, but to listen to your stories and tell their own. Part of the way in which religious education is deficient is in the way it tells the stories: the children don't have a chance to take the story into their own lives and make everything around them a story. Things that are obviously stories are passed off as "real" and children are punished for "lying" when they create stories out of their own lives.

When your bright-eyed child comes to you with some whopper, it's a story if it has narrative. It's a lie if you ask a direct question and the eyes roll as the child tries hard to think up an evasion. Most religionists don't distinguish between stories and lies. They often confuse them. Jesus is a story, but a real story. Going to the store and seeing a tornado fly all the cows away is a story but it's a lie. Seeing Jesus might be a story which the kid knows is a story, but the teacher says is true.

The only way to treat the age of story telling is to look for the narrative. The only way to deal with lies is to eliminate the punishment. Don't get me wrong, kids are devious. My niece at the ripe old age of two decided that she didn't want to go to sleep in her crib. She managed to pull the vacuum cleaner into the crib and covered it with a blanket. When my sister went in to check on her she was frightened by the fact that the little girl wasn't moving and discovered the vacuum cleaner. After a big search, they found her in the closet with a flashlight and her toys. Craig went through a thieving phase around the age of four. I caught him slip gum into his pocket once at the store. Rather than accuse him, I told him that if he needed gum so bad that he had to steal it, we could buy it. It took the thrill and the danger and the fear out of stealing.

The Santa story has narrative. It is a story. My sister tells a wild, exaggerated tale of her tennis club almost getting burned down. It has narrative. It is a story. Your kid starts telling these wild tales at kindergarten about how you fly away every night in flying saucers and he really heard the noise of their jets. It has narrative. It is a story. Even if the teacher complains to you about how your kid lies all the time, it's not a lie. Get the teacher to apologize to your child and tell her to look for narrative before she confuses creativity and practicing narration with lying.

So much confusion happens during this imaging, storytelling phase. Some children are very literal and very dramatic. My nephew got his parents called into school because of the wild tales he told his friends (the teacher overheard) of the way his parents beat him and tied him in his chair in his room. He also told stories of Mike the Friendly Tornado because a tornado had touched down near their house and his mother had almost lost her mind with fear, but Mike the Tornado was a story and the Evil Parents story was perceived either as a lie or a secret confession of abuse.

This confusion shows up all through communities who have a rigid story telling routine. It is exaggerated in societies where stories are a borrowed cultural event and not innate to the culture. It shows up in places where "real" stories exist. There are no "real" stories, no "true" stories. There are facts. There are accounts. But stories are never "real." Kids know this as well as they know that a stick is not a "real" gun. The key is to know the form. If the violence is exaggerated, dramatic, well-conceived and repeated in a ritualistic form, it is acting out a feeling. If the violent behavior is spontaneous, often accompanied by tears or piercing howls, or hidden, it is an attack. If the lie is stylized, has a beginning-middle-end narrative, and the speaker holds himself like a strutting cock (look at me) then it is a story. If the lie is an evasion to a direct question or confused or muttered in a voice that is not meant to be heard, the child is protecting himself from punishment. The lie of defiance or the calm lie of scorn is a trademark of the older child.

My family is Irish. Tall tales are not only expected, but if you can't relate the happenings of the day in a way that is exaggerated, hysterical, and completely engaging, then you're a fool. Craig's father's family are strict Lutherans, Prussian Americans with a solid work ethic and a serious attitude. For them, an account of the day should be like an account, dry, exact, and easily verified. Teach your child the art of story telling and you may find that your child finds Christian and New Age stories boring. Stories are like advertising. The object is to entertain, teach a little, and to transport the child into another world. Exposing a child to stories is a way to handle the religious indoctrination.

"Mom, today Granny told me about Easter."

"Um, was it a good story? What was the story about?"

"Oh, he was some dead guy that actually wasn't dead. It was kind of boring."

So much for Jesus. She might have got a little more attention had she told him that Jesus was a zombie... filled with gaping wounds... and... to this day... insane people still eat his flesh... ooohoohahaha!

"Mom, today we learned about Santa Claus."

"Oh, was it a good story?"

"Sort of prissy."

"What if the reindeer were velociraptors instead, would that make it more exciting?"

Wild giggles. And then a crayon drawing with Santa getting eaten by velociraptors. So much for Santa at our house.

Chapter Six

The Voice of a Marble

When my sister was little, she talked to marbles. When Craig was little, he had imaginary friends. My nephew had to line up all his cars in a certain order so they could go to sleep. I have a friend who changed personality with costume. Around the story-telling age, children learn to model others. They suddenly realize that if they hit Rover, it might feel like it feels when *they* got hit. This is the age where mothers begin to yell, "What would it feel like if I took your toy away from *you*? Now, say you're sorry!"

Modeling is a human characteristic that is very advantageous for life in groups. It has survival value in that mothers need to model what their infants are feeling. Modeling leads to the more difficult cognitive functions of abstraction and multidimensional imaging. But modeling at this age can drive a rational person crazy. The first step in modeling is not usually sympathy, but anthropomorphizing.

Primitive religious celebrate conscious life in everything. The New Age people see consciousness everywhere. They don't eat meat because of their sympathy to animals. Trees think and rocks think, only very slowly. They call it a celebration of life, but it is a celebration of returning to ancient religions. People who are good at one-layer modeling make good New Age converts.

People who are good at one-layer modeling also make good candidates for guilt. Remember that mother yelling at her child? Once children can do modeling, they can be manipulated by guilt. Mothers depend on this. Christians thrive on it. Show pictures of starving children with big eyes and the pocketbooks empty. Show pictures of sad-eyed puppies and the pocketbooks empty. "You're just selfish!" is

29

the cry. It's an accusation that you don't know how to model.

There is a new rage about something called Emotional Intelligence. It brings modeling skills to light and disparages those who show no sympathy for others. To be emotionally intelligent means that you know what others think by modeling how they feel. It means that you have the magical gift of sympathy and compassion. It means that you'll pick up that little stray cat and nurse it back to health. It means, as a child, that when Molly gets hit, you'll be the one to cry.

When Nancy went to kindergarten, her mother warned the teacher. "If Nancy ever does anything bad just hit the kid next to her and she'll be good the rest of the year." She was so proud that Nancy was so sensitive. Nancy was the dream child of the Christians and the New Agers. So sensitive. So sympathetic. So malleable. So guilty. So eager to please and unburden her terrible, terrible guilt.

Men are often astonished to find how vulnerable they are to guilt if it is wielded by a woman. Oh, the tears. Oh, I've hurt her. Oh, what can I do to make it better? Oh, buy you something to apologize? Certainly, honeycups, just tell me what I can do."

"You've hurt Mommy's feelings!" is the New Age moms' cry. New Age dads try it, too, since New Age dads don't have to be tough.

So the child talks to trees, sees fairies, and cries when Bambi's father gets shot. Good Atheist material? You may do what my father did and throw up his hands in disgust. Women! But now the boys have to cry over Bambi, too.

Guess what? It's bullshit. Some people are immune to guilt and tears and bullshit. But there is a better way to teach your children than to "toughen them up." The problem is not that modeling makes good, guilty godmongers out of the sensitive, but that the modeling is not learned, but imitated. When people imitate modeling, they imitate the action of putting themselves in the other person's "moccasins." But when, oh when, do they see their parents or teachers demonstrating the art of putting yourself inside the other person modeling being in your moccasins? Or the art of modeling him modeling you modeling him?

Is your brain starting to hurt?

Yes! It's difficult. That's why people don't do it. It's the long division of the world of "emotional intelligence." Just as the religious people don't want you to unravel their "proof" of the existence of a supreme being, they don't want you to model them modeling you. Did you, as a child, ever start the joke of thinking about thinking about thinking about thinking? Did the very people who seemed to be good at modeling start screaming at you to stop it?

There is no survival value in modeling a baby modeling you. You don't need to. You project yourself into the baby and think of all the things that could be bothering it. Simple. Effective. End of story.

But look at that woman who is crying because you "hurt her feelings." She's asking you to model her. She's chiding you for not modeling her. She's depending on your ability to model her pain and feel guilty. But don't stop there. Model her modeling you. No, not her feelings, but her projection of what you are feeling. Is she modeling you?

Ask your child who talks to cars to think of how the cars think of him. He can imagine how the cars feel. Can he imagine how the cars think *he* feels?

Are the buzzers going off in your head? If people are not modeling you, they are not interacting with you but with a thing. If children model something that cannot model them, they are interacting with a thing. The consciousness is only directed one way. Persons who are manipulating are recognized by the way in which you, as the victim, are supposed to do the modeling, one way, at them. Pictures cannot model you, but someone can tell you to model some projection of reality into the picture.

"Aah, the poor thing!" is a plea for you to turn on the modeling tools.

This phrase should immediately forewarn you that you are going to be subjected to manipulation. You are being told in advance what the moccasins feel like.

Many people are burned into pride by the way that the object of sympathy wakes up and bites them on the hand or spits in their face. They have not modeled the "object" modeling them. They have not asked for information to construct a model of modeling.

Back to old teary eyes. If you ask her "what do you think I am feeling about the way you are feeling?" the answer will not be an answer. You'll get accused and told how to feel. If you were to ask the religious nut "what do you think I think about you?" the answer will not be a real answer. It will be a repetition, an evasion, or an accusation, or some other trick to manipulate a "hard sell."

The only cure for children who talk to everything is to teach them how to model deeper. Ask them if they think that rocks are alive. It's hard to use "conscious" at this age, but this is a good age to introduce the concept. If they say yes, rocks are alive, then counter with "do you think the rocks think you are alive?" They might get a little puzzled. "Can a rock tell you that it thinks you are alive?" No. They might listen and say, yes, but this means that they think you are starting a story. But the idea will stick with them after a time.

"Can you think about the dog?"

Yes. "That is what it means to be conscious."

"Can the dog respond to you, can the dog do some action to get your attention?"

Yes. The dog begs. "Then the dog is conscious; it is thinking about you."

"Can you think about the tree?"

Yes. "That is what it means to be conscious."

"Can the tree deliberately get your attention?"

No. "Then the tree is not conscious."

"Can your teddy bear deliberately do something to get your attention? ..."

When your child has conscious and not-conscious under the belt, introduce the idea of modeling. Walking in someone's shoes. You may not have to do it since our culture is really into walking in everyone else's shoes right now.

When children have a firm grasp of this, start them thinking about what the other person is thinking about them thinking about him.

Interrupt situations where one mom starts using one-level modeling as a means to inflict guilt. Use yourself as a demonstration. Ask the mother if she is putting herself in the shoes of your child having to put herself in the shoes of the other child. When the reaction is indignation or pride, don't try to push it, but make sure that your child sees it and marks it. As soon as the situation is over, ask your child if the guilt inflicter answered with an honest answer or was there an attempt to lie.

It may take years for your child to catch on. It may take minutes. Either way, you've saved one more person from the machinations of guilt.

We have a saying, "to grant humanity."

This means to interact with others as if they were human, like you. To model them modeling you, on and on. This means that you do not fall into assuming that you know what they are thinking or feeling. Require people with whom you interact to grant you humanity.

Chapter Seven

"Now I Lay Me Down to Sleep..."

For the first time in history, babies and small children are sleeping alone. Not only has this practice established itself as convenient, but it has permeated the moral fibre of Western cultures to the point where the family bed is some kind of sexual taboo. Yet, most parents do relent when a child is terrified from a nightmare in the middle of the night, until it is a repeated event that is seen to be manipulating the parents. Again, I cannot stress enough that small children are not manipulative, just interested in having their needs met and their fears alleviated. The parental practice of "toughening up" children smacks of Puritan or Calvinist asceticism and – as seen in the anthropologist Ashley Montagu's studies – dangerous.

There is a telling scene in Kurt Russel's new movie, "Soldier", about a boy in the future who is indoctrinated from birth to obey and kill people, where a woman asks Todd, the soldier, if he feels anything. "Fear and discipline, Sir!" he finally exclaims. This man is so afraid you can see him shake any time he is faced with his fear. Kurt Russel is frightening in how well he portrays this terrified boy in a man's body.

The New Age movement swings the opposite way of the Calvinistic "cult of toughness" because life today is easy compared to life in those times. Everyone is encouraged to be sensitive. But the dictates of culture, especially the moral dictates of the "religious" side of culture do not operate for the individual, but for the greatest good for the most people. Religion is interested in saving humanity from itself at the sacrifice of the self. Whether you view fear as a weakness or fear as a sign of sensitivity, fear in a child won't go away because you want it to.

34

Nighttime tends to bring on fears. Darkness, isolation, and quiet all combine together to make the child's imagination go haywire. For five years I ran an institute that studied dreaming and REM sleep, and many of the people I saw who were completely debilitated by nightmares were completely ordinary, competent, rational people. These people were so terrified of going to sleep that lack of sleep had wrecked their lives more effectively than if they were insane.

I am always taken aback by the death/sleep imagery in many religions. The little prayer that is supposed to comfort children is terrifying to them. But the idea is not to think about the prayer, but they repeat it over and over until it becomes a kind of mantra to repeat, a litany for bedtime.

"Now I lay me down to sleep, I pray the Lord my soul to keep.

If I should die before I wake, I pray the Lord my soul to take."

I find it's ingrained in my mind along with the theme song from *Gilligan's Island*. I can't forget it. I cannot tell you how many nights I lay awake, petrified with fear that if I closed my eyes I would die and "the Lord" would take me.

With my own son, I encouraged him to do math once we turned out the lights. Now that he has his own room (yes, children naturally want their own beds at about the age of five) he is permitted to have a bedside lamp on. He is frightened of the dark. Always has been. For years, we have lain together in the dark – he in his pj's with his stuffed animal of the week, and I trying not to fall asleep so I could get back up and get something done, and talked about math. Sometimes a recitation of the multiplication tables would lead to some discussion about a problem. Kids seem to open up more about their personal lives when you're lying next to them in the dark. We also would discuss the future and his plans and other things to pull the focus of life into what would happen tomorrow.

If it's inconvenient to sleep with your small children, try to be flexible about staying with them while they fall asleep. Often, even older children who have become reluctant to openly show you how they feel about you will fall asleep with their arms around your neck. Along with fears, the dark and the night bring out affection. I feel sorry for parents who want to yell at their kids to go to sleep because they miss out on this affectionate gratitude and that sigh of security that makes the whole parenting mess seem worth while. Ending the day on a positive note is good for everyone.

Nightmares come and go. In nightmares clinics it is known that nightmares cannot be battled after the fact. Religionists big on guilt use nightmares as a "proof" of sin. New Age people use nightmares as a "proof" of the existence of other dimensions and miracles. Out-of-body experiences are a form of dream. So are UFO abductions. So are many visitations from angels or demons; so are many accounts of travelling to strange places. The yogis have made an entire practice of dreaming.

Dr. Stephen LaBerge of Stanford University proved with EEG that lucid dreams do in fact exist. Lucid dreams are dreams in which dreamers are self-aware and know that they are dreaming. Around the age of story-telling children may start to have lucid dreams. It is difficult for them to separate dreams from reality until about ten years old. Lucid dreams, in which dreamers have all the faculties of smell, touch, sight, and hearing – all as though they were awake – are almost impossible for a child to distinguish from reality.

Jack, who is now almost seventy, is a typical lucid dreamer. He is a retired Air Force officer, a quiet man, who has never spoken about his rich dream life. When he was five, he began having terrifying, reoccurring nightmares in which he was being chased by a giant mouse. His brother naïvely said as children will do, "Why don't you just turn around and chase the mouse back?" Jack did just that, not knowing that he was not supposed to be able to control a dream. Not only did he get rid of his nightmares, but his dreams became his own private "holodeck" where anything he wanted could come true.

If you're skeptical, check out the EEG traces and the experiments done by Dr. LaBerge. He has a web-site at www.lucidity.com and several books still in print. Dreams play such a large part in religions, that as an Atheist, you must not ignore them. Give a logical explanation and a child will not have the miracle of dreaming to sustain a faith in the occult against all reason by the light of day.

Another kind of dream is called a "false awakening" dream. In REM, the body goes into paralysis. During a false awakening, dreamers dream that they are awake. They get out of bed and see their bodies lying on their beds. They panic and then find that they are paralyzed, back in bed, and they feel as though they cannot breathe. Often, they jump out of their bodies again and will sometimes feel intense fear that they cannot get back inside their bodies. Thousands of people report sensing a presence, sometimes malevolent, that is waiting for them. When dreamers really awaken, they often are convinced that they have had an out-of-body experience. If they have a false-awakening dream where they start floating around the room like a dis-embodied spirit, they may then find that they can go through walls, observe people theyknow, shoot out the ceil-ing into space and encounter "God." The variations of the dream content are infinite.

This is a common dream. Hardly ever is it viewed as a dream. Hundreds of people are convinced by the reality of the dream that they have been somewhere, out of their bodies and seen their bodies possessed by demons. There are hundreds and hundreds of such accounts. Often the dreamers are so afraid of the paralysis, thinking that it is a real sign of some pathology, that they become terrified of sleeping.

We had very little success trying to convince these dreamers of the unreality of a dream. When I finally had a lucid dream, I found that it was as different from regular dreaming as watching TV was to riding a roller coaster.

The only way to deal with a nightmare is for the dreamer to deal with it *during the nightmare*. This means kids, too. As a parent, sit down with children who have awakened from a nightmare in the middle of the night and explain that the dream is theirs. They can make the dream do what they want. Children before the age of ten, readily accept the idea that they can control their dreams and do. It is only adults who think that this is nonsense and will not accept even the data to prove that control is possible. The nightmares will not go away. Tell children that the nightmare will come back, but that they can change the nightmare. They can call Daddy into the dream. They can make the monster into something they like. They can sprout wings and fly away from the bad guys. They can do anything. That is the "magic" of lucid dreaming.

Dreams do not belong to religion any more than morals do. Dreams are not in the realm of UFOs and fairies and psychokinesis. To try to convince a child that dreams don't exist or that they must be ignored because they are not real, is opening up your child's mind again to the hooks from religion and the occult. To give the child the gift of lucid dreaming cures nightmares, makes sleep a fun place to go, and brings into the light of things human that which has always been pushed back into the mysticism of the paranormal. Preparing your children for the fear of a false awakening does away with ideas they may have that they were abducted, possessed, or molested – all common in reports to this day. Give your children the edge of knowledge.

Chapter Eight

The Demon Within

This chapter of the book may seem to you to be a strange way to attack religion. I don't claim to attack religion so much in this chapter, as to give you an insight, as a parent, into the way in which your child may be infected.

Historically, the study of personality has been polluted and monopolized by religion, pseudoscience, and the occult. Astrology seems to have the throttle on any objective studies of temperament preference or behavioral differences. I want to present to you, as a rational parent, a way to take back knowledge of the self from the mystical cults that want to sell it to you or your kids. Giving children a scientific way to understand their differences will keep them from being tempted by the search to discover why they are unlike others into falling prey to religious and occult traps that depend on the differences between people to make them fear alienation and the fear that they might be "broken."

In two independent studies it was found that personality is comprised of categories of polarized preferences. The two personality maps that were based on actual observation and interview are the Myers-Briggs Type Indicator (MBTI) and the Berkeley Five. The MBTI is widely used in the military and in many professions. In the Berkeley Five, all the personality preferences discovered in an international study were found to correlate with the MBTI except for the preferences of *Feeling / Thinking*. The Berkeley group used four traits instead of two, separating *Emotivity* from *Consideration*. The MBTI puts *Consideration* (people orientation) and *Emotivity* in the *Feeling* preference and *Selfishness* (object orientation) and *Reserve* in the *Thinking* category.

Small children are born with temperament built in. In the school years the preferences for learning and application of learning become more pronounced, and in the teen years the final preference for time management becomes very pronounced. In this chapter I will stick to the first category in each of the tests, that of "source of energy."

Carl Jung was able to describe the differences between Extroverts and Introverts without using name calling. In each person, he saw that there was a preference for one kind of behavior over another, but that the other kind of behavior was not dormant, but internalized. He called the preferred personality preference the "dominant personality" and the internalized personality preferences the "auxiliary personality." An Extrovert is a person who uses the dominant personality for social interaction and in dealing with the outer world. Extroversion is the preference, whether a strong preference or a mild preference, of sixty-five percent of Americans.

An Introvert is a person who uses the dominant personality for introspection and analysis of the effects of outer phenomena on the mood, thinking, and reactions of the individual. The auxiliary personality is relegated the duty of social interaction and dealing with the outside world.

My own theory, from having watched a family of mostly introverts from infancy and from talking with other introverts, is that babies born with an abnormal sensitivity to external experience must be introverted in order to manage the noise of the environment to a level at which they can perceive and react to it. We think that it might have to do with a tendency for the brain in these infants to have a heightened sensitivity to sensory input or a lessened inhibitory capacity. Whichever it might be, the result is that the infant is often on "overload."

Introversion results in "fussiness," "fearfulness," "nervousness," "clinginess," and an inability to "shut down" or "tune out" the world. Where an extroverted baby is one whom everyone can hold, who smiles and coos and loves attention games like "boo!" and "tickle-tickle," the introverted baby is often seen as difficult and demanding. This is the baby who bursts into screams when grandma tries to hold it.

The reason for needing to understand the social limitations and the style of introversion and the inner limitations and style of extroversion is that they seriously affect how your child will be seen by others. Because introversion is a lesser known preference and because severe introversion is a despised quality that is seen by religions to be anything from "demonic possession" to "an evil, antisocial attitude," part of protecting your child – in the school and on the playground, as well as from religious ideas – is to understand these preferences.

The first sign of introversion in babies is that they will scream to break your ears if you put them down or they will "fade" into listless apathy. The extroverted baby will be vocal but easily distracted and amused. Extroverted babies are happy as long as the world is interesting, their basic needs are met, and someone is making goo-goo eyes at them. They are willing to try anything from eating off a spoon to flicking at that set of plastic keys you wave in their face. They mimic well and love "talking" to Mom or other members of the family.

Introverted babies will have one caretaker. Maybe, by the age of three months, they might accept another person – but only if the primary caretaker is in sight. These infants will be unhappy about a thousand things you cannot guess – from the feeling of what you think is a "soft" blanket to the doorbell going off and startling them, to the sight of a strange face. In mothering groups, the extroverted babies are all on the floor, fascinated with the older children as if they can't get enough. The introverted babies are clinging to their mothers, hiding in their hair when anyone talks to them, screaming if they are put on the floor, or in the arms of the poor mother who has had to leave the room because her baby is on overload.

There is almost nothing about the introverted baby that is desirable to a new mother. She is admonished to "control" the child and to let the baby "cry it out." Her heart breaks, but she is deeply afraid that her little bundle is broken. It doesn't get better with the toddler. Extroverted toddlers are the ones who can mimic everything you say at eighteen months. They happily career around the room, love the play group, and happily go shopping or to a babysitter. They poke their fingers at everything including the dog and have to be in the middle of all the excitement. The limits of extroverted toddlers are tolerated. They need to be told "no" repeatedly and often must be pulled away from trouble. They hate being alone or still or sleeping. They hate it when you talk on the phone and will storm and rage if you don't give them attention. They repeat everything all day long until everyone is tired of the "parrot."

The introverted toddler is a mother's nightmare. She tries to take the girl to play group and the child screams and clings to Mom as if the floor were burning. When approached in the store or on the playground she bursts into tears of terror. She rages at her inability to describe her complicated inner states. She is particular and will often scream if she is given jello instead of ice cream. She is so sensitive to textures and sounds and light that the world is her enemy although her curiosity will drive her back again and again until she is utterly exhausted.

The introverted boy is uncontrollable, unsocial, seldom verbal, often sickly or fussy, but he will sit for hours and look at a book or happily plonk with blocks in a room where he can hear you talking on the phone. His attention span is way beyond his years and he seems determined to master everything without getting distracted. If you tell this child "no" once, the lesson is learned. Often mothers make the repeating error with this child and the result is misunderstanding and tears.

If these children are admonished and feel angry, they will get secret revenge and, years later, you might discover that all your art books were ruined. These are the children that parents do not understand and who will not communicate. Extroverted children will announce everything that happens and happily recount for you the day's events.

Introverted children are the ones who, when asked what they are doing, say "nothing."

Introverted children have massive problems in school. Severely introverted children number only about one in one hundred. Nine times out of ten the child getting beat up or called names is introverted. Children seem to be able to smell fear, and the schoolyard is an introverted child's worst nightmare. Grade school and pre-school teachers are seldom introverted. Studies show that introverted children need almost five times longer to respond to a question. They have to process the question, and rehearse what they will say under the pressure of extroverted children wriggling as if they would pop, with their hands as high as they can keep them. Their greatest fear is in being the center of attention, and their preference is to hide in the corner of the class and hope not to be noticed.

Teachers are accustomed to having to beat up extreme extroverts because they cannot listen and will get into trouble because their hands and their mouths can't stop. Teachers will try to tell you that an extrovert has attention deficit disorder. They will try to tell you that an introvert is depressed or has avoidance disorders. Worried parents will try to force the introverted child to socialize. This is the worst thing they can do. Introverted children get the impression that shyness and fear are shameful and that their parents hate them.

Three of the "seven deadly sins" are sins of introversion. In another personality map based on pathology, no less than six of the thirteen types were "disorders of introversion." Six of the ten commandments involve crimes committed more often by introverts. New Age religions have resurrected the image of the shaman, a traditional introvert. If your children are introverted, they can learn to be social, but they will never, never be comfortable with it. This becomes a sign that they are broken, and they will search for a way to fit in, a way to alleviate the pain of being a misfit. These children love the story of Rudolf and the island of misfit toys.

Religions prey on misfits just as predators will cull the weak out of the herd. The call of seclusion is attractive to these children. A lifetime of meditation in a safe place is just what appeals to them. Parents do much to help an extroverted child keep interested in hobbies or friends. They brag about how many friends they have and how well they do in school. Extroverts are charismatic, lovable, and wear their feelings openly.

Beware of accounts that an introverted child won't participate, gets nasty when pushed, lies, is an underachiever, is unpopular, cries all the time, shows a tendency to ferocious, evil, uncontrollable violence, is sarcastic, is uncooperative, openly despises everyone, gives up everything when threatened, tries too hard to please, or is sneaky or evil-minded.

When given a supportive environment, introverts really shine. They learn well, they never forget, they are loyal to a few friends, they can even become interested in overcoming shyness to become insightful and gentle therapists or understanding coaches. Introverts will save humanity from the excesses of not taking the time for self-examination. Their sensitivity can be an early warning system for environmental excesses such as noise pollution. The computer industry is almost one-half introverted. These people have changed society in places like Silicon Valley, where it is acceptable to break off engagements without having to explain and people often beg off social activities due to being "peopled out." The dress code of casual to slovenly is theirs – along with the Internet. These are the scientists who are so into their work that they can work for days and never talk to anyone or go outside. No, it's not unhealthy. It's just a preference.

Before you suspect that your child is a victim of religious prejudice, take a look at the kid and wonder about the possibility of introversion being the "real" reason. Many extroverted children seem impervious to criticism or will reply with a taunt or a fist and all is settled. But extroverted children fear being alone, so they may not speak out against rampant religious ideas for fear of losing their friends. They will mimic all the songs and sayings happily, blithely because everyone else is doing it. Before you recoil in horror at your child repeating some Christian dogma, take a look. Is the child extroverted? If so, it may only be a chant as meaningful as "red rover, red rover" and as harmless. Punishing children for accepting a chant or prayer is trying to take them from their friends.

I have this strong memory of my nephew riding his bike in the street when he was about five. He called as he rode around and around in circles, "Oh please, oh please come be my friend! Oh, won't you please be my friend! Please be my friend!"

You'll note that Jesus is everyone's friend.

Also note that Jesus is unconditional love. The introvert thinks, "Finally, someone who will accept me even if I am broken."

Note the double doors of all religions. One door is for extroverts. They covet the parties, the temple filled with people, all friendly and sociable. They love the glitter and the tapestry of religion – the laughter of all the candles and the fact that everyone is all together. They can meet hundreds of new people. All they have to do is walk past the holy house on the holy day and all those people are smiling and talking and laughing.

And then there is the quiet, solemn, peaceful side of the temple. The echoing hugeness of it. The far off chanting and the quiet. There is the call of the esoteric side of religion, the way to know the inner face of the god. Years of study are required and then the novice is awarded the inner sanctum, the inner circle where there are few and he or she is unique among them.

Every religion has these two faces. Even the buildings. Befriend that social child who needs a friend. Protect that shy child who needs an inner sanctum.

Part Two:

What Am I?

The School-Age Child

Chapter Nine:

The Price of Confidence

Children learn differently. If you argue with a religionist, you may be facing a different language. As long as you are muttering away in "Greek," the message is lost. If you understand the differences in the way people can hear, understand, and communicate, you can translate and get a real argument instead of a battle of wills.

If you can recognize the learning styles of your children, you will know how the deists will filter the information to them, or rather how they will learn it. If you can fight their learning on their turf, you are way ahead of the game.

Time after time, people never really communicate and finally throw up their hands with the "he's just too stupid to get it" lingering on the air. Often in battles with a spouse over a child, the battle is simply a communication issue. Once the translation is made, confidence is restored and work can actually get done. If you talk to children in their language, they will have confidence in their own ability to learn and confidence in you. This is crucial because you, as an Atheist, are presenting the argument. They will learn to be a deist from everyone else. If they understand you, then you may win yet.

Humans do not merely imitate, they learn. They do not have to rely on instinct, they can learn. They do not have to be victims of the nature of the world and themselves, they can learn. It becomes apparent early on how a child will want to learn. Do not make the mistake of thinking that yours is the only way to learn. Every teacher they have will push their own way of learning. There is both a German and an English notation for the calculus. You get the same answers in each notation.

Learning has two extreme polarities in styles and people usually map somewhere in between them. Like extroversion/introversion, there are extremes of style and more tempered styles. Studies show that the more intelligent the child, the more extreme the style becomes as the child approaches adolescence. After adolescence, the extremities fall off with more and more tolerance for and ability with the "opposite" style.

This is the breeding ground of word humor. A sense of humor has proven to be a person's best defense against brainwashing. This is the place of greatest frustration and the greatest prejudice. If you have worked in a large company or in an institution, you will start to nod your head as I describe the preferences.

There is one learning style that is popular among sixty-five percent of Americans. The MBTI calls this preference *Sensing* (S-type). A misnomer, perhaps. The other pole is named *iNtuiting* (N-type). Basically, the S-type relies on gathering the particulars and, through induction, drawing conclusions; the N-type imagines hypotheses and, through deduction, comes up with instances of example. On one side is the brilliance of Sherlock Holmes; on the other is the brilliance of Einstein. On one side is the methodical plodding of Elmer Fudd; on the other side is the wacky imagining of Wyle E Coyote. Notice that every time Elmer fails to catch the "wascally wabbit" he just keeps plodding with his gun and his hat. Every time the Coyote fails to catch the Roadrunner he goes back to his blackboard and dreams up some new scheme. The idea is that, like Bugs, your children can be fast enough to dodge either approach.

The time-honored way of learning is to memorize the facts. "A, B, C, D. . ." sings the child. "One, two, buckle your shoe!" Children shine at this age if they have a strong preference for seeing what's before them and remembering the order of things. Taxonomy is their passion. "The head bone's connected to the neck bone!. . ." They have an eye for detail. Hands have fingernails when these bright children draw a stick man. They love the way in which the world is an orderly procession of things. Look! Here's how to tie a shoe. Look! See, I'll show you. Look! You try it. Over and over and over again. Practice makes perfect. What happens at 6:00? Right! Farmer John has his dinner. This is the house that Jack built. This is the mouse who lives in the house that Jack built. Ninety-nine percent of grade school teachers are S-types. They teach in a traditional style which has not changed in two hundred years. Rote, remembering, and rhyme are their tools. And the rhymes are sticky. Names of things stay the same for a thousand years. The calendar and the seasons and the days of the week are all traditions that will be so old one day that no one will remember why the names are so. "What is today, children? Today is Tuesday! And what do we do on Tuesday? Right! First we do coloring!"

The church has you beat here. Face it. If your child needs rote and tradition, the churches have anywhere from 8,000 to 2,000 years on you. All of culture reflects the passing of the holidays of the church. Each holiday has a story or stories. Each season has a rhyme about god. You are going to throw rocks at an 8,000-year-old edifice that is so ingrained that even the days of the week have the names of its gods. The Soviet Union fought for two generations to undermine Holy Mother Russia. The camp is entrenched.

If your children need directions to take a bike apart, give them directions. The place where the gods haven't had such a heavy hand is in mathematics and science. Start getting these children interested in all the names of the leaves and all the names of the stars and all the names of the rocks and all the names of the bones. Show the way in which plants are classified and rocks are classified and which animal has this hoof and which animal has this horn. Your little Sherlock will soon proudly announce, "No, grandma, that's not a deer! That's a springbok antelope! No grandpa! That's a grass, so it must be a monocot!"

These children love mysteries. They love puzzles that are procedural or based on identification. They love the rote and ritual of chess and other board games of strategy. They love the finiteness of numbers. Theory and imagination are not the gifts of these children. When arguing about gods, do not retreat into intangibles or theory. If they start leaning to the rhyme and the tradition of religion, fight back by filling the gap of knowledge with more orderly systems. They will easily prefer the logic of math to the mystery of gods.

The other children are the ones who talk to rocks and believe in ghosts and tell a stories that would make Dr. Seuss pale with envy. They are all over the place. A bit here, a bit there... directions? What directions? Let's just dump out all the pieces and see what new things we can build! Fix the bike? Why can't we make a time machine instead? These children will never learn to tie their shoes but they'll figure out a new way to wear them so they don't have to tie them. Remember Einstein? Remember the tale he tells of how bad he was at math? Such children will understand multidimensional topology but won't remember the way to go home. Well, we'll just drive around until something looks familiar!

Boredom. BOREDOM!!! An extreme child will even find the alphabet song BORING! Sing it backwards or upside down. Food is BORING! Let's eat our peas through a straw. Sleep is BORING! Let's hang upside down off the bed like a bat. Clothes are BORING! Let's put our pants on our head. This child will turn to Atheism, because it goes against tradition, but will also be in love with ghost stories and UFOs and miracles – and anything else that isn't traditional. Chess, okay. Let's pretend the queens have to go under the table and secretly attack the other guy. Math? Yuck! BORING!

Teachers hate such children. They're the ones who will make up a thousand-and-one variations of the Pledge of Allegiance – and if they're shocking, so much the better. They're the ones who could care less if *cat* is spelled c-a-t or k-a-t or c-a-t-t or k-h-a-g-h-t. When told to write a paragraph using no adjectives, they will write a paragraph using all adjectives.

But there is a key. The theory has to come first. The question has to come first. If these children can get a purpose, they'll suddenly (and in lightning-fast time) know everything there is to know about all the ingredients for their project. "Let's build a computer" turns into learning everything about electricity, circuit diagrams, engineering, and anything else they have the patience for. It'll be all over the place and not very methodical learning, but it will fit within some framework in their own minds.

Religion preys upon their imagination. Miracles are for the benefit of such children. So also the pantheon of talking animals, angels, fairies, gods, devils, evil messages when you play the record backwards, the kabala, the visitations, the burning bush, all and everything that will make life on earth a little less BORING!

If creativity scares you a little, and you believe that anything that isn't broken should not be fixed, you're in for a long haul with these children. The battle for the elements of rationality will be a losing battle. These children need theory. They breathe it. They need their lives to be filled with interesting parts of projects. They need to have room to make monsters and supermen and fairies that change color when the weather changes and space aliens that replace the president with a robot.

There is only one fix: back off. Such children scorn authority. Point out the authority traits in godmongers instead. The last thing you want to do is to set yourself up as an authority figure against which they can rebel Give them every book and every story you can find that is weird. Get them into magic tricks and theatre. Teach them riddles and puns and writing upside down if the penmanship homework is BORING! Give these children a copy of Houdini and let them design a new board game or build a new kind of go-cart. Let children invent new foods to eat and new ways to eat them. Change your house into a chaos of a laboratory and a circus. There is a need to experiment, invent, concoct, and destroy. If they realize that you are not going to make them be BORED! they will gradually start to ask you for advice about projects. If you can feed them information fast enough whenever they have some hare-brained scheme, they will learn that some things work and most do not.

Your worst enemies – their wild imaginations and short interest span – will become your best ally, although not at first. But as the tedium of schooling convinces them that most people are not worth listening to, they'll stop listening to the "traditional" way to do it. Let them reinvent those Bible stories. Later they might read the book in the original Greek or Hebrew and see for themselves all the contradictions. They'll be the ones who will call some preacher on some obscure bit of dogma remembered from some book on ancient Sumer that was part of some project done perhaps twenty years ago for a study about ancient visitations by UFOs. Not many deists can deal with the authority-hating brilliance of the creative mind.

To learn the language of your child shows that you care enough to reach out a hand and honor his or her abilities. To undermine style with constant harangues about being slow and stupid, or flighty and having no concentration, is useless. It will cause self-esteem problems that will set you at each other's throats for the rest of your lives.

Knowing that the time is 7:52 exactly and not "around eight" is not being stupid or obstinate or overly careful. Knowing what the time is on Venus over the Mons Persephone is not being silly and deliberately irritating. One will be grateful for a watch that shows microseconds and the other will be grateful for a watch that shows the time all over the world. The gift of the watch is being a parent; the gift of time in the form that appeals is being a friend. Better yet, give them both a book on exotic fish. One will be fascinated with the names and which is which, the other will be fascinated with the weirdness and the differences of adaptation. Be exacting and meticulous with one and original and questioning with the other and you'll end up with Bugs irreverently poking at all the dogmas.

Chapter Ten:

Is it Fair or is it Just?

Susan was in third grade when her class began to discuss the planets in the solar system. One boy drew a picture that showed Jupiter being bigger than the sun. The teacher thought it was very nice and showed the class. "But Jupiter isn't bigger than the sun," Susan protested. "It might be," the teacher said, patiently trying to prevent a fight. "It is not!" Susan cried. She was horrified and indignant. She was appalled that the teacher would support a blatant lie. She felt betrayed. "Now, now, Susan, just because you believe that the Sun is bigger than Jupiter doesn't mean that Johnny might not think so. He's entitled to think how he wants." "But he's wrong!" Susan screamed. The teacher stood up and made Susan go to the back of the room in time out for being hostile.

The third preference of personality is that of emotivity and application of learning. This is where the battle gets ugly. Even the two tests split here, the Berkeley Five giving *Emotivity* its own category. MBTI describes one extreme as *Thinking* (T-type) and the other extreme as *Feeling* (F-type). Loaded words. Berkeley Five has one extreme as *Excitable* and the other extreme as *Reserved*. The other category is polarized into *Self-sacrificing* and *Self-serving*. Wow. Still loaded.

Basically, the two extremes are preferences in how learning comes to be applied. One side applies learning to objective goals; the other extreme applies learning to cooperative situations. According to MBTI Americans are split 50/50, with gender as the decisive factor in ninety-five percent of cases. This is where popular literature can create pseudoscience with personality. *Men are from Mars, Women are from Venus* is the example that comes to mind. It is a whitewash of the issue, but has just enough truth to cause the fires to be lit to start melting the pitch.

I suspect that most Atheists are the T-type. I also suspect that many of them have spouses of the F-type. Many of the battles fought in the classroom are with teachers who are of the F-type and parents who are of the T-type. "Interfering" grandmothers, do-good teachers, "sensitive" friends, and the self-sacrificing message of religion conspire to put rational and justice-seeking Atheists on the warpath. Too often, the child is caught in the middle, forced to choose between mother or father.

Rationally, objectively, and skeptically Atheism is the only logical course of action. The contradictions don't hold up to the scrutiny of the trained mind. Religion is anti-life, anti-progress, anti-technology, and anti-freedom. All right. So why are you having this fight? Why don't your cool and dispassionate arguments hold any weight with your children? Why do your children end up cast out when they try to stand up the for the truth?

Because the playing field is wrong. You're using a knife to eat peas. You look ridiculous doing it, too. All the peas fall off but you keep insisting that the peas are just not the right shape to stay on the knife. Keep talking in that cool and logical voice and wonder why you feel like you're speaking Chinese. Your adversary will let you ramble on and on and be oh, so tolerant of your selfish, cold, logical, dispassionate, argument that has no grounds in reality.

So, you're a teacher. Three little girls are having it out on the playground. Two against one. Do you stroll over and coolly say, "Now, now, children. This isn't right. This is not being very productive." Or do you run over there jump into the middle of it, pull the girls apart and shout, "Stop it! Mary, Rhonda! You're being bad! Two against one isn't fair and you know that! Now what did Jennifer do to make you girls attack her?"

If you have to do this often enough, and if you spend most of your time concerned about teaching children how to be fair and consider each other's feelings, then in a Susan situation, you will see a fight and break it up rather than see an argument and try to point out the truth with logic and objectivity. In later years when the ratio of male teachers is higher, you used to see the opposite problem. A girl would feel that the situation in a math class was unfair because she was being baited by her math teacher, who was trained to used all the techniques of argument to get his students to see the point. The girl would burst into tears, sure that she was under attack and the teacher would roll his eyes at the idea that he was a "bully" and dismiss her from the theater as being emotional and "stupid." She was. She was trying to use a spoon to cut her meat. She misinterpreted the playing field and misunderstood the rules where the pursuit of truth and knowledge is the goal and all behavior is oriented to reaching that goal efficiently, swiftly, and without distraction.

Deists specialize in the tactic I call "bait and swap." They lead you into what you think is an argument about justice and turn it into a fight about fairness. They start off with an appeal to mercy and cut to the quick with a defense of logic. Constantly, people are baffled and hurt by the ability of some to "switch the playing field" in mid-game. And then there is the on-going problem of one person playing on one field and the other on the other field and no one has realized that the two are not the same.

Sports is where most men learn about fairness and abiding by the rules and hurting the opposition and defending the weak position. It is only when their children become sick or threatened that most women become aware of their own ability to pursue a goal without regard to the people involved. What mother would consider a doctor's feelings in preference to the health of her child?

If you are facing a woman (the situation does not depend on gender) who is playing for your child's future on the playing field of social situation, the appropriate argument for Atheism is an appeal to the health of the child. Not to her mental health, to her physical or emotional health. There is a whole cast of bad guys out there to put in the place of the disease carrier. You want to teach your daughter to be skeptical of religion because so many women have been killed or died at the hand of the church. Cite some tale of a young woman being burned for being a witch. Cite a pitiful tale of a woman dying in Mexico because she was raped and could not have an abortion. Get creative, but stay with a SITUATION, do not back track into the generalities of the history. Use names. That really helps to make the issue less abstract and much more real. If you know someone in common who was a cult victim, this is even better. Make sure that the girl who was abused by religion was of similar age to your daughter and make sure the story is really disgusting and pitiful. You've got to present a case where Mary and Rhonda are beating up on your little Jennifer. If Jennifer is a boy, use all the horrible history of abuses in the church. John must be in danger for his life or he must be threatened by a specific, emotional trauma that will damage him as a father.

If this "woman" belongs to a church in which she has had bonding experiences and feels secure in the specific history of this church, you must remove the discussion from the arena of this church's influence. The victim must be drawn specifically, but the church should be a vague, but real, threat. Your child is the victim, but all enemies have faces for women. You must seek to keep the face of the enemy vague and cruel.

Because of the unfortunate fact that gender and this preference overlap to the extent that they do in this country, rational girls like Susan will automatically be seen as starting fights when they are outraged by a slip-up of justice. Women who do not meet the stereotype still fight with not being taken seriously, having their arguments dismissed for personal reasons, and often find that women attack them viciously because they see a logical, unemotional, intelligent woman as a possible person who will see people die rather than be a peacemaker when the issues are at stake. In motherhood, such a woman is a threat to children.

Men who value fairness and find that they are good at managing people have a little more leeway, but are often not trusted as being able to fully evaluate the situation the way that women can. Men mistrust their ability to do what is right for the project and see these men as "muddying the waters" and "slowing down progress." American men who have had to go oversees often suffer culture shock when they deal with Asians who value fairness and consideration far above the thing they are manufacturing. Companies in Singapore and Taiwan are seen as inefficient and impossible to work with.

When fighting a situation in school where the playing field has been switched on your child, or a teacher has misinterpreted an action, or other children are baffled and threatened by behavior by your child that does not match the conditions of the game, look for a way to teach the child to use a knife or a spoon. A child who is comfortable in both environments will be adept when the deist baits and switches on her.

At this age, Susan should be able to learn that the teacher will see situations where she is right and the other child is wrong as potential "beating up" situations and will act accordingly to protect the underdog. Susan should be encouraged to try to change the situation into a "Why can't we help Johnny out with some pictures from a book" and to offer herself as an instrument of aid for the good of all rather than an instrument of argument for the enlightenment of all.

If the teacher sets an example of a child being an intellectual threat, the other children may ban together to protect themselves. As on a playing field, they will be proactive and try to cripple the opposition before one of their men is down. Although it requires bravery on the part of the child, it is helpful to relate the story of Mike, the chimpanzee who beat on the garbage can lids and won himself not only a place back in the troop, but alpha-male status. If the victims can provide for the pack a way to get at grownups through a gross story or some other kind of childhood rebellion, they will win the appreciation and respect of the other kids. Even Catholic kids love to see dirty pictures or hear gross tales of gore and zombies. No child is going to stand up for the religion of the grown-ups in front of a pack all oohing and aahing over something taboo. On the playing field remember that it is acceptable, albeit not really fair, to sling mud at your opponents. "The minister wears leopard skin briefs when he digs in his backyard" is the level at which the fight is aimed.

Your child can also win by being creatively distracting. "Wanna see a dead snake?" is a surefire way to prevent getting beat up at recess. Who cares about religion and what is right and wrong when you can go see a dead snake! Even if the snake is not really there, by the time the chase is on and the snake is discovered to be "missing" and all the speculations have been made and the accusations denied, then recess will be over.

Once children learn how to distinguish problems of fairness from problems of correctness, they will be able to practice skills that will help them overcome fights and arguments with all their emotions intact. When harassed by a lot of religious children all ganging up to "bully" them with the "facts" from the Bible, they can realize that it is time to get out the big guns and shoot down those facts. If it suddenly changes to name-calling and emotional tirades, they then will be able to switch and start tempting them to break out of the confines imposed by those evil adults.

My son is a scathing Atheist. He has yet to be beat up at school, even being an introvert and weird. He has a wacky sense of humor, an appreciation for gore, a wild imagination, and plenty of "let's go see a dead snake!" appeal. Occasionally, he has had a very literal, well-meaning teacher whom he has despised. He has learned to be patient with them and sees them as being inferior and to be pitied and tolerated with a kind of noblesse oblige which flatters and irritates them. He still has problems with loud gym teachers because he hates team sports (they're too organized) but is able to understand that what he hates is less than what he enjoys. I asked him if he talked to his buddies about god-questions. He replied, "It's a good thing we have computers so people have something to do besides talk about boring stuff like god." A bit naïve, but a good start.

Chapter Eleven

The Shill Game

The only cure for advertising is to sit down with children and start them on the path of taking things apart. Religion does not stand up to the skeptical mind. Working with a child over the world of advertising is good practice for working over the world of myth and imagery.

I knew early on that there was no way I was going to keep Craig from television or cultural stories like the Santa Claus myth. I knew that the cure for both was a lot exposure from a critical perspective. I sat down with him and watched cartoons. "Look at that, Craig," I would say when GI Joes started to parade on the screen. "Can you tell me how they get those army men to look more fun than they are?" Well, give a child a way to take something apart and your house will get demolished. Craig had more fun figuring out how the commercials worked than he would have had lusting after the toys.

When approached with a new toy wish, my first comment – instead of "no" – is "well, tell me why you want it." This puts children into a position where they have to prove their case; sometimes they prove to themselves that maybe they don't want it.

Craig and I also spent many hours in toy stores playing with the demos. This took time. But when a child starts whining for this, that, and the other fantasy, that takes time and energy, too.

It has been known for some time that the best resistance to brain-washing is a good sense of humor. Elmer Fudd is easily hypnotized, but Bugs is less gullible. I have an Atheist friend who says that you can learn a whole lot more about people by noting what they won't laugh at than by talking to them. All the major religions warn against taking their god's name in vain. Humor helps the skeptical mind, it helps develop a sense of the ridiculous, and it teaches the ins and outs of word play.

Aristotle talks about humor quite a bit. He stresses that humor should be aimed at the ridiculous. Shakespeare was a master at horror and of the ridiculous, both good weapons against faith. Humor is a release and humor is healthy. Many religious people have no sense of the scathing nature of sarcasm, and deadpan parodies can make talking with them a stitch. I admit to having a weakness for baiting Christians and New Agers. Movies at our house are rather like "Mystery Science 3000" where the two robots and their buddy rip into old B-grade sci-fi movies with no mercy. Lampooning has always been the enemy of religion. Even the Catholics had to tolerate All Fools Day to give the people the release of humor.

I think, if you do one thing only to protect your children from religion, that giving them a sense of humor might do it.

Santa Claus and his reindeer are maudlin and a little intimidating to the sensitive child who wants his presents. Santa Claus getting eaten by velociraptors was not something I found terribly funny, more gross, but all the little boys in Craig's pre-school were howling over it.

Jesus is a great, pompous idol to poke fun at. Given the reports of his own words, he had a pretty good sense of the ridiculous, so poking pins in his idol is probably something he also would have enjoyed. Jesus's followers in the form of all those black frocks and silly hats are even better targets.

I usually ask children to take a Bible story and make it funny. Funny to them, not necessarily to me. It will keep you and your friends in stitches to hear some of the responses, but maybe not for the same reason the kids are in stitches. I've seen kids pee their pants over some joke about the Easter bunny in space or Jesus getting buzzed by flying saucers or other, irreverent, lovely nonsense. Another way to demolish the power of the little Christian songs is to have your kids invent a rowdy version with different words. Whew! Those get around. You may have a bunch of parents down your throat for teaching their little angel an "enlightened" version of "Jesus Loves the Little

Children." This will go way further to demolish Christianity than your child trying to preach to their child.

Children love body humor, but they also love to make fun of everything. I'm afraid that if you decide to teach them humor, it will go all the way. Everything will fall under the scythe of humor. I like a house full of wise-cracking, smart-alecky kids, but some parents find that it bothers them. Craig has discovered that when he gets sarcastic or irreverent in his grandmother's house, she starts to cry. He looks out for her though, and tries not to make her cry, but secretly thinks that she needs to loosen up and give the old belly laugh. She does on occasion and becomes a very beautiful person. My father sometimes grumbles about teaching kids respect, but I think they respect things that they find respectful when given permission to put anything under the gun.

Humor develops a sharp mind. Sensitive children may find it cruel and terrifying to be the brunt of humor, so jump them up and start them off poking at their own things until they get the hang of it. Humor easily gets abused, so be prepared to referee fights through humor. The battle cry of "Mommy! Brian called me a toad face!" is countered with "Well, what is *he* then?"

Nonsense rhymes and babbles are great protection against the hypnotism of religious mantras. When a child is fluent in nonsense, he easily picks up the "hail Mary, full of grace" and turns it into nonsense. "Flail Harry and fall on your face" or "Mail Mary and maul 'er with mace" defeat any power these litanies have. Forever. We all find that the Hari Krishnas are the most comical of people. Their chant lends itself to all kinds of lampooning.

Yes, you are helping give birth to a troublemaker. In my opinion, minds are for making trouble. It's creative and it keeps us free from religious tyranny.

The other great trick you should teach your children is the art of sleight of hand. One of the weapons of religion is "bait and switch" or distract the audience while you fleece their pockets. Teach your children to understand the art of the con. Look at those commercials. All that lovely imagery and then, way in the corner, the logo. Every child should read a book about Houdini and any books you can find on the history of scams and cons and hoaxes.

The point of this education is so that they will recognize a con when it comes in the form of Scientology or some more obscure cult or merely in the form of a friend saying "let's get our fortunes read!" Show your child how vague and wide open to interpretation the horoscopes are. Let them try to dupe you. Let them try to dupe their class-mates. Once burned, a kid might be more skeptical in the future.

Sixteen-year-old Nancy was accosted on the street by the Scientologists. She smiled to herself and agreed to go and be "interviewed." She was asked if she had any over-whelming problems in her life that she felt that she needed help with. She smiled and said, "nope."

The Scientologist was flabbergasted. "What do you mean you have no problems?"

"Well," she said. "Sometimes I procrastinate on my homework."

He leaped on this and made it into an entire reason for her life being a complete mess. She let him run on and then blithely asked, "how can procrastinating on my homework possibly make my whole life a mess? You guys *want* my life to be messed up so you can fix it, don't you?"

The man avoided her eyes and she knew she had caught him with the card up his sleeve. She couldn't resist playing the game back.

"Hey," she said loudly. "Sorry about that. You know I could make *you* feel a lot better and it wouldn't cost you as much as you're paying these creeps."

The man blushed and looked around to see everyone looking at them.

"You're a minor! Get out of here!" he hissed.

She laughed and was glad to leave the stuffy office. Up to that day, Nancy had never heard of Scientology or that thousands of intelligent people lost fortunes to that brand of church, but she recognized the shill game.

Chapter Twelve

Learning the Odds

When children have already had their hands in guts for a time, when they can start to come to grips with time (they start telling stories), when they can start to model others (they start talking to walls and sinks and animals), then they are ready for the subject of animation and deanimation. Hopefully, at this point, you've had the cat-pancake experience. Usually the experience at this stage is the death of Rover or Fluffy or Goldie when the child is in school.

"What happened to Rover?"

Religionists avoid an answer and revert to the "Doggie Heaven" mantra. The real question is "What happened to Rover?" Notice that the religionists don't answer the real question. They always use a potentially traumatic situation to push in a fix just as they use a rebellious situation to push in the punishment.

Find a flip-book or a book about film. The what of death is not in the body, it's in time and movement. Ask a child to define a movie. "What is a movie?" "*Move*-ie." "Something that moves." Run the flip-book. See, it's moving. Freeze the VCR. It's not a movie, it's a picture. What's a body? It's like a picture. What's a human? It's like a movie run on the VCR. The movie is life. Death is when the electricity fails in the VCR and the movie cannot run. Pull the plug and urge the child to try to run the movie. No amount of button pushing will bring back the movie.

If you have a very smart child, you'll be asked why death is not like sleep. Why can't we just plug in the cord again and bring back the movie? Death is when the pictures get so damaged that when you put the electricity back on, the pictures are messed up and the movie will not run.

Explain that some diseases cause the film to get damaged and then the movie doesn't play right. Explain to the child that without the "electricity" the body starts to decay inside right away and gradually decays all the way through.

So Rover lost his electricity, he lost his animation. Now his body is too far damaged to start him up again. Think of other ways you can give a metaphor for death. An electric car is good. Break the car's wheels and it is like having a body that won't work. Take out the battery and the car is dead. Explain that science has not yet figured out how to recharge the batteries of a living thing.

But what if the question is not "what happen to Rover", but "what did you do with Rover?" This is not a plea for Doggie Heaven. This is asking permission to say "goodbye." Americans are not good at grieving. They want to protect their children from grieving. In their rush to protect the child, they are usually over-reacting.

Laura's dog got run over when she was seven. Her father was grief stricken. Laura wanted to say goodbye to Sage. "No, no, Laura," her father said, his eyes full of tears. "Sage is dead and you shouldn't see him." Laura was stubborn. "I want to say goodbye!" she insisted. Her father relented. Laura walked up to the dog patted his head and told him goodbye. Her father choked back his tears and looked at her in wonder.

Often, parents mistake a child's motives. Children are often offended by a breech in the rules at this age. If someone is going away, the proper thing to do is to say goodbye. Grade school children are concerned with rules and procedures and customs. They are also often cruel in their honesty. If you are sad, to tell children of this age otherwise makes them think that you are insane or hiding something from them. How a child reacts to the loss of a pet depends upon temperament at this age.

Emotional children may need to grieve, and if you give permission to grieve or share grief it will be bonding and beneficial. Less demonstrative children may need a simple closure, time alone or, if they are more heady, a discussion about the situation. Let the child lead. Above all else, do not enforce an emotion on a child or try to suppress an emotion in a child. If your reaction to grief is different from the child's, explain. A simple explanation like "I don't like bad feelings so I try to distract myself until I feel better" is far better than forcing the child to grow up and take it "like a man."

This incident may also lead to a question about the death of a parent as children begin to project specific situations and draw parallels. Craig hit me with this question when he was about eight.

"So what are we going to do about this death thing, Mom?"

"What do you mean, Craig?"

"Well—" he was uncomfortable.

"You mean you don't want me to die?"

"Yeah, that's it."

"Well, you and I come from a very long-lived family. They may have a cure for death by the time we get old."

"Great. That's a relief."

I could tell that Craig had been worrying over this for a long time. The loss of a parent is a worry for some children. Fortunately, we live in a time when there may be a chance that life extension research can push back death. Conveying to the child that there is a possibility of beating death is important. If there were no fact of the matter then it would be a lie. If it were a fact, that would be great. There *is* a chance, and I think that conveying the urgency and the difficulty of the fight to eliminate death gives both challenge and substance to this discussion.

At this age, many children face losing a grandparent and are aware of other deaths in the family. You may run into the "Why did Grandpa die," question. So many times this leads to a discussion about "God's will," and fate, and heaven. This simple question is a request for the particulars of death. Not until the child is a teenager will the morality of a particular death over another and the quirkiness of fate be an issue.

The answer depends on the disease or the accident. No more. I have never met a child who wanted to know "why

Grandpa and not Grandma" once the facts are straight. Explain disease. Explain old age. Use the film wearing out example if you need to or the battery running down. Often the child will then think that everyone who is sick will die. A discussion of the odds of accidents and the facts of illness and recovery is a necessary discussion at this point.

If children become concerned about the possibility of accidental death, there is a simple way to convey the odds. Ask them to think of one out of one hundred and then to count up (help out if needed) all the people they know. Rarely will they know one hundred people. Ask them to help you write down all the numbers from one to one thousand. This should take a few hours. Then tell them that the odds of dying in a car accident are something-to-one. The odds of getting a fatal disease are something else-to-one. Tell them that the last big disease that killed one in ten people was a hundred years ago. Then you can go into a discussion about minimizing risk and wearing seatbelts, etc., etc.

Godmongers make a big show about chance. They depend on the fear of chance to inject uncertainty into life. This creates a fear which their god can alleviate. If some religionist tells your child that there is a chance that one of his parents will die, and he should get them to believe in his god so that they will go to Heaven, he can ask what the odds are of one of his parents dying. If the godmonger is foolish enough to get specific and say 1,000 to one, which is pretty exaggerated, your child can imagine just how big 1,000 is and wonder why the godmonger is worried.

The deist may counter with the fact that everyone dies and your child can look at him with a puzzled expression and say, "Why? Isn't medicine going to wipe out death?"

If the godmonger starts talking about the unreliability of medicine, the child can answer "why aren't you spending money for research to make it more reliable? I think you *want* me to die."

Chapter Thirteen

Rites and Rituals

Do you cover your mouth when you yawn? Do you believe in demons? The gesture says that you do.

Our lives are rich with symbol, superstition, and ritual. As Americans, this problem is aggravated by the fact that American English is the most idiomatic language in the world and has borrowed vocabulary along with custom from all European and a hundred other countries. Our language is historically so unique that the vocabulary itself is a map of a history of conquest. Anglo-Saxon words and customs were defamed by the Norman French, Gaelic words and customs were defamed by the Romans and, later, the English. So many innocent gestures and words were turned into images of the Devil's hand that it is almost impossible to speak logically or rationally without using the language of the conquering church.

Here are some examples. The word *guilty* is a Norman French spelling of an Anglo-Saxon word which meant "responsible" or "authored." It was a positive acknowledgement of having "willed" something to happen, or taken steps to a successful conclusion of an idea. The words *witch, wicked, wit, wizard, wisdom, guide,* and *witness* all have the same root in the word for "to know" or, more accurately, "to direct or guide." The words *holy, healthy, hale, whole, Hallow(e'en)* and *hello* all stem from a desire for health or wholeness. Well-wishing among the Anglo-Saxons involved the use of the middle finger, called, literally, "the finger of health." Try raising your middle finger now and see how many people interpret it as a gesture of goodwill!

The point is that we are steeped in history, as shown by gestures that have been condemned by foreigners, words that have migrated from their original meaning, and superstitions that have no bearing in modern reality.

If you cover your mouth when you yawn, you are keeping demons from entering your body. Throwing yourself prone or bowing in prayer is an ancient gesture of subordination to the top monkey to leave you alone. Gaels fought in chariot formations of twelve men including drivers. The thirteenth man was a man who was one too many, unlucky enough to be chosen. The spirits run about loose at Hallowe'en merely because the Celts operated on a thirteen-month lunar calendar and it was forbidden for contracts to extend into the next year. A yearly review of contracts and agreements took place on the extra day at the end of the year. The Celts started their year and their day with the departure of the sun. The Harvest month was called "Hallgmonath" (month of health) by the Anglo-Saxons, so the extra day before the "holy month" or Hallow's eve when unfinished business was displeasing the ancestors and the wisemen.

Rituals and holidays were complicated long before the Christians took them over. Still, many people want to "clean up the act." Fundamentalists forbid Hallowe'en and Christmas trees. Jews resent the confusion of the Festival of Lights and Passover with Christmas and Easter. Chefs prepare dishes of pork and beef instead of pig and cow. "Hell" merely means "place of light" and was a generic underworld, but, to Christians, all those pagans are going to be there.

But the Christian god still looks like Zeus and we celebrate his day every week on "Wotan's Day" or Wednesday. Mary's day is Friday, or the day of Fricka or Venus. So why haven't the fundamentalists made up their own calendar and days of the week? Why haven't you? Are you still covering your mouth when you yawn?

Yes, it's silly to try to unravel every word, every gesture, and every ritual that we use in order to purify our minds from the taint of religion.

Children love rituals because of several reasons. It helps them get a grasp on time. It helps them feel that they are alive in a stable, well-ordered, universe. It helps them bond with a common language to the rest of society outside of their immediate families. It helps them look forward and look back. The stories help them learn association and the intricacies of metaphor and imagery. And rituals are fun. They involve costumes and parties and good food and presents.

I advocate a strategy of *laissez-faire* when it comes to holidays and culture. I don't tell Santa stories to threaten my child, but I don't keep my child from Santa. In a way, I am lucky. Hallowe'en is the major holiday in three generations of my family and birthdays happen to fall there. So Christmas is anticlimax. But my son spends the entire year planning his costume – rather like the little boy, Jason, in the comic strip *FoxTrot*. He's big on "Goosebumps" and doing detailed descriptions of monsters and demons for his "Dungeons and Dragons" games.

Has his fascination with the undead and the demonic ruined his ability to think? No. Has it made him credulous of accounts of "real" demons? Absolutely not. The late astronomer, Carl Sagan, admits to believing in UFOs and all kinds of alien stories as a child. He lost his belief rapidly when he grew old enough to do his own investigations. He became the greatest UFO skeptic on the planet. When the poet, Robert Graves, researched his famous work, *I, Claudius*, he found evidence of a real "king of the Jews." But his book, *King Jesus* would have him burned by almost every Christian on the planet.

Understanding involves two procedures. The first one that children learn is the gathering procedure. The second one they learn (or don't learn) is the discriminating procedure.

Young children need to gather. Give them stories, holidays, cultures, and the names and pictures from natural history. They love stories about fairies, but they also love all those dinosaurs. Add rituals and holidays to the pantheon. Make up your own rituals for marking time and making parties.

Have a cowboy party every year. See the rodeo and have a cowboy party. Let children mark the calendar for the annual cowboy celebration and read them stories about the

Old West and show them all the different bridles and cattle brands. Have a masquerade every year on the off season. This will win popularity for your child at school, because kids love costumes. Call it the "Summer Solstice Ball" and stay up all night for the shortest night of the year. Have dance contests or contests of wrestling and throwing and other summer sports. Put off lights and pull out a cake for a "Walk on the Moon" party and watch a video of the first moon walk. Celebrate all the birthdays of the explorers and scientists.

Give your child memories of childhood. This will fill up the gap that religion seeks to fill. It will make your child "holy" (*lit.* "full of health") and the "holiness" of other families will not be so attractive. Children who are exposed to all kinds of stories will not latch on to the story of the Easter Bunny because they're starving for stories. A market with only one booth gets all the business.

Pain and grief do not go away. But the way to counter them is to make them seem smaller by comparison. They become a little bit of grief, rather than a universe of grief. It is a healthy sign in people when they do not dwell on pain or guilt. Religion has to fill a void, and to do this a void must be there.

It may not be until the teen years that children start to cut away at all the "bullshit" they have learned. Again, it creates a void if, when all is cut away, nothing is left. Science is so rich that all children who learn botany or astronomy or zoology will have much to fill their lives. There are thousands of accounts in history that will be more marvelous than most religious stories. Give your child Lief Erikson and Grainne O'Malley, the Pirate Queen. Accounts of Ghengis Khan and Marco Polo, stories of Galileo and Tycho Brahe, romances like Abelard and Heloise, mysteries of Houdini and Volta. Let them in on the excitement of the race for the moon and the search for electrons. Give them the pageantry of Robert Louis Stevenson, Jules Verne, and Victor Hugo. There is magic in Thor Heyerdahl and Antoine St. Exupery and the exploration of the world. Let them experiment with kitchen chemistry and garden botany. Let them see medicine in the folklore and growing of herbs. Where does aspirin come from? What is digitalis? How are dyes made? Give them real technology and have them build a car or a plow or a fort.

If you depend on school to provide wealth for your child's mind, you are doing your child a disservice. Children need adults to participate with them in the search for knowledge. Most teachers have thirty or more students to control and little time or money to teach with. But telling children what to do is not what children want. They want the participation and the process of going through the motions.

Have a box car race every year. Spend the winter building cars with your child. Teach about tools and wood and mechanics and eventually motors and the physics of aerodynamics and propulsion. I am amazed at how many parents don't want to learn – and then they wonder why their children don't want to learn.

Make a ritual out of a weekend meal. Teach your children how to participate in the purchase of food and the making of courses and the decoration. Make it a kind of party and encourage a creative child to dress up. Have a Mad Hatter tea every month complete with little cakes and all kinds of herbal tea drinks.

It's not the subject that matters, it's the performance, the preparation, the anticipation and the participation of the family. If Grandma is invited to a tea party where everyone must wear wacky hats and talk backwards then Grandma is very busy trying to help with the party rules and has little time for telling your child about Moses. But if you are a lazy parent or a busy parent, then your child will turn elsewhere for parties, rituals, and the decorations of life.

My son is very big into costumes as I said. I used to have a kind of "intellectual salon" every few months where parents could bring kids. It was potluck, but because it was a "party" Craig had to make a costume, which meant that I had to make him a costume. One time he was Anubis when he was going through an Egypt craze. Once he was a tiger, complete with wired tail and real claws. Once we spent two days making a dragon's head out of *papier-mâché* with a tongue that he could move from inside the mask. He remembers every one of these costumes with great joy because it was something we did together.

For a child in the gathering years, give things to gather, don't try to take things away. Children will remember things you gave them over things they had to do on their own. I have wonderful memories of spending hours with my father, who was a chess master, walking through end moves and studying opening gambits. The memory of chess with my father is more special to me than memories of Christmas.

Chapter Fourteen

"Do You Believe in Fairies?"

Parents feel that they lose control of children in the middle years due to peer pressure and school influence. Abusing children's limited ability to model, pressuring them to do what the group is doing, and using guilt to make them feel responsible for things outside of their control runs rampant in these years.

The scene in *Peter Pan* where Tinkerbell drinks the poison meant for Peter and then Peter has to get the children in the audience to clap to make Tink well, is an excellent example of the abuse of all three of the above. This scene is a great filter to understand if another adult will be able to encourage insanity in your child or your child will be victimized by the psychomanipulation.

There are many elements of *Peter Pan* which are religious in nature. There is the aspect of death. Tink dies and is brought back by the children's faith. Captain Hook is threatened by the crocodile. No one ever grows old. There is the call to belong. The Lost Boys are a band of misfits guided by Peter and mothered by Jane. There are the "bad guys" who had no mothers: the pirates. There is the Devil, spirits, Peter's own image without a shadow, anthropomorphized Evil, and miracles.

But *Peter Pan* is quite irresistible. "We can fly!" is just too attractive.

The New Age movement does not guide children into one faith. It demands that children accept all faiths. No longer is the story that the world must only be 10,000 years old because the "begats" in the Bible prove it, but that the world lives on the shell of a giant turtle, and the world was created by Coyote, and the world's origin is every myth ever created by man, including the "myth" of paleontology. To cry for adherence to the "story" of evolution is being intolerant of other people's stories. Education, epistemology, and metaphysics all fall into the court of fairness and consideration for the other people of the Earth.

Mythology and stories provide satisfaction for two avenues of human frustration: wish fulfillment and understanding the self. The New Age movement is an attempt to acknowledge that there are universals in humanity. Where the New Age movement fails is in separating the desire for something with the accomplishment of something. Everything is relegated to "wish land" and the greatest "saints" are those who can demonstrate that "wishing makes it so."

Stories like *Peter Pan* expose desires in children. The desire to fly. The desire to live without adults. The desire to mother. The desire to defeat one's enemies though trickery and guile. The desire to rescue a dying friend by clapping.

To defame *Peter Pan* is to invalidate these desires. Doing so is suppression and makes the desires forbidden and all the more desirable. Children see the world of adults as one of privilege. Adults have money. Adults can do what they want. Adults have a house and food and toys. Adults don't have to obey. Adults aren't afraid of the dark. Adults can drive places all by themselves.

What child doesn't yearn for a world where children have the power of adults without having to be adults? The crashing disillusionment of teens is that they get betrayed. The world handed to them is not the world they saw as children.

You can help children by helping them to understand that their desires are valid, that you do not have all that they desire, and that they can gradually gain some of what they desire, if not all.

The desire to fly is universal. Some people have said that it has to do with a desire to return to the womb or some genetic memory of Cambrian life in the sea. Research into paleontology and comparative anatomy makes it appear possible that humans evolved out of the trees, into a shallow sea which is now the Rift Valley, and then onto the plains. It is a controversial theory, much overlooked and despised, but worth examining. The leading proponent of the "Aquatic Ape" theory is Elaine Morgan. Watching babies swim underwater is like watching someone fly. Any child who has not learned terror of water loves to swim. I think this desire to fly is well-founded and should be encouraged with swimming, and looking forward to the adult activities of soaring, going into space, scuba diving, and sky diving.

Answering this desire is not scorn for the idea that people can fly, but an acknowledgement of your own childhood desire for flying – that kind of fear/joy of jumping off of things or running fast and holding up your coat over your head in the half-nonsense that the wind could make you fly. Giving flying some reality, like sailing, ice sailing, soaring, ballooning, snorkeling or swimming lessons will make the imagined attempts seem less attractive.

The desire for a tiny friend that only the child can see is universal and has roots in the psychology of humans. A child who gets a firm grip on fairymania, might be satisfied with making dolls, or collecting dolls, or making marionettes, or writing and drawing stories of a microworld. Looking at the world makes a child think of being a giant. This is normal since children live in a world of giants. The world of the miniature is fascinating for them. It gives them the power of parents in being big. It gives them the satisfaction of being responsible for something. Pets will cure some desire for a fairy friend, but pets grow up. You can acknowledge that children want a world of their own by helping them create and explore the miniature world.

Building elaborate houses for little dolls is a wonderful activity. It doesn't cut out the fairy play, but it gives reality to life of the small. Designing houses for mice is better. Ignore the anthropomorphizing of the mice. Part of it is acute observation and part of it is wish fulfillment. The real problems of feeding and keeping the mice from escaping are real enough to persist in the child's memory longer than the idea that they are little humans. Some children like fish and snakes and other miniature worlds.

Death will be a part of the pet world. It won't be possible to make Tink live again, although the child will desperately want to. We all want to. Who wouldn't wish for a drug to give to sick loved ones to make them better? The desire is real. The study to bring back the sick and dying is a life-long activity. Make the clapping real. Give children the real world of advances in medicine and the mechanics of life. Pretty soon, they'll be scoffing at the New Age faith healing and will be passionate about a *real* way to counteract death and disease.

The desire to be among the Lost Boys is a very real human desire. The answer to this desire is easy. Let the child make a club and a world to "club" in. Forts, treehouses, cellars, and attics can become places forbidden to adults, brothers, sisters, or other outsiders. Encourage the creation of elaborate rituals and costumes and ghost stories and sleep-overs and secrets. Recognize that a big part of this activity is trying to do things adults don't like or won't do. Give children "forbidden" things to do like mark each other with tattoos using wash-off markers or letting them use make-up to make their faces horrible. Let them design "haunted houses" and mazes only large enough for a seven-year-old. Give them a recipe for a secret brew that is written in code. Give them a book on codes and sign language.

They are going to tell their secrets and giggle about you behind your back. But the importance of this reality is that you can't join. They can't join your world, so they love taunting you with the fact that you can't join theirs. Look forlorn, but give them the first clue to a treasure hunt for a chest of hidden cookies and they'll think you're "the coolest, Mom!"

Everyone wants to fight the "bad guys." Giving vent to a world where there are the good guys and bad guys is older than religion. Creating a leopard in the shadow of the trees will keep your child happy for days. Hunting is no longer a PC sport, but it satisfies this need in a big way. Safe games like laser tag and spontaneous childhood games like "tag" and "king of the mountain" exercise the desire for there to be a bad guy. Introduce children to comic books and encourage them to draw their own comics and write their own stories. Costumes are an important part of this play. Batman remains one of the big favorites. The great thing about the imagination is that the bad guys don't have to be "real." Most of this game is in the preparation, the costume, the persona, the weapons, etc., but encouraging a real combat sport like karate is often very happily accepted.

Barbie, princess play, cowboys, astronauts, Peter Pan: the world abounds with wish fulfillment. Rather than dismiss wishing as "irrational," use the wish as a means by which the child can reach into the real world. It may take them many years, but sometimes children can surprise you by becoming serious inventors, famous writers, or karate champions.

Chapter Fifteen

"God is great, God is good..."

I'm in favor of people taking responsibility for their own values. Among the religious, no one owns values and no one chooses values and no one has to be responsible for values. The religious almost always despise the use of money to convey value, so I like to use money as a means to "objectify" value. Money does what a god cannot: it conveys value both ways. It makes people responsible. It allows for responsibility to be easily traced, and it takes emotion out of the discussion.

Yes, I know this is controversial. Distrust and distaste for money is one of the last holdouts of the religious mind. Many people who will rant about freedom of thought give not even lip service to the talent of money to facilitate communication of value. "Money is evil," they say. They expect to convey and enforce their set of values by the fact that they are bigger, older, and have lived longer. Now if science was so authoritarian, wouldn't someone say something about it?

You value keeping your house clean. It protects your things, saves time, and makes you feel as though there were order in the world. You have a child who is untidy. You yell and yell at him to pick up his things. His room is knee-high in toys and clothes and bits and pieces of his life. You are disgusted and offended by his behavior, yet yelling at him just makes him sulk around and maybe pick up a few things and look at you like you were asking for the moon. Reasoning with him won't break his habits. Harassing him will make him resentful and dependent.

Let's bring money into the picture. You can say, "All right, I'll revoke your allowance!" Money has become a weapon. There is no exchange of value here.

For there to be an exchange of values, for money to act as money, it must flow both ways. You can say, "All right! I'll pay you a dollar to clean your room!" Well that's a step. The next step should be either, "Give me ten," or "I'll pay you a dollar to let me keep it messy." Rarely is this second step met with anything but anger and a dismissal. The second offering is so offensive to most parents that it is seen as insubordinate, threatening, and hurtful.

But what has really happened? The child is trying to communicate to you through the dollar. If you keep talking, there will be an exchange of value, and, hopefully, a win-win situation.

"I find that it makes me feel that everything is slipping into chaos and that you don't care about the things that you own, so I wonder if I can pay you to keep your room clean."

"How much?"

"How much is it *worth*?

"An hour of your time on the market is probably worth about five dollars. But do the job and I'll pay you ten. Keep it clean and I'll pay you five dollars a week. Any more than an hour a week cleaning this room and I would see you as being lazy and wanting to hurt me by taking advantage of my valuing a clean house."

"How much do I have to pay to keep it messy? It makes me feel comfortable to have it this way."

"I don't know."

"Ten dollars a week?"

"No, a messy room is really an affront to my need to keep things from getting lost and broken. Maybe the price of all the broken and lost things, plus the wear and tear on the furniture and your clothes and maybe the price of my time to remember to close your door and pick up your things in my rooms. I'd say a hundred dollars a month"

"Wow. I don't have that kind of money. Why can't I get a hundred dollars a month to keep it clean?"

"Because maintaining something costs less than replacing it."

"Oh. Okay. Ten dollars now and five a week."

"If you can't manage it then you'll have to pay me for my

time to do it. If you do it the first week and I do it the second then we're at zero. Agreed?"

"Yeah, that sounds fair."

In this exchange the child has learned something about what his parent values and why. He did not turn off when his mother started to talk because he had something to gain and to convey in the conversation. By taking responsibility for her feelings and needs and values, the parent has effectively conveyed that it bothers her, not that it is somehow something everyone expects and accepts. She is showing the child that her values are important to her and not just to society.

Money doesn't have to be the go-between. Yet in highly charged emotional situations it helps to clarify the real issues. Bartering is just as effective. "Clean your room once a week and I'll spend an hour a week doing something you want me to do" is equally effective and communicates the same thing. The key is that whatever is exchanged, time or money or favors, the exchange is two-way and negotiable.

This exchange so quickly takes value out of the realm of the "expectations of society" *i.e.* religion, that families find that they spend almost no time at all fighting over values and that their kids develop an appreciation and trust for their parent's opinions.

We developed a rule of thumb about what children can take responsibility for and when. At seven, children can clothe themselves, do their own hygiene, set their bed-time hours, and choose their diet. Responsibility does not mean choosing and not accepting the consequences. If the diet choice is candy, the mother can expect the child to pay for the teeth and the effects of sugar. I'm amazed at the lack of faith parents have in their children's ability to know what they want and what will happen if they do so and so. At the age of seven, children can be made to shop for their own food and learn to spend money for that food in the store. A desire for a new dress can mean that the child gets to choose not to get something else.

Once children learn responsibility and understand something about the consequences and limitations of choices in the real world, it's way easier for them to understand them in the world of human interactions, values, and the limitations of action. Children who know that their parents respect their person and property will not cave in very easily to violations of their person or property by others, even the indirect violations such as pressure to donate to a church. Children who can earn money and respect and can complete a job are far more immune to the "might is right" fist in the velvet glove of guilt and social conformity.

This is also a very valuable step in learning authorship and free will.

Sometimes children are baffled by the invisibility of the hand of authorship.

Food arrives on the table. God gets the thanks for it. Where has the child seen Mother earn the money or the food being grown or slaughtered – or even the exchange of money at the grocery store. The food is just there. The clothes are just there. The toys are just there. Magically given to us by someone – why not a god?

Growing a garden, even a windowsill garden, is an excellent way for children to understand about food. A visit to a farm to pick fruit or vegetables is a great lesson. But watching a plant grow from a tiny seed, if you water and tend it, gives value to the food that comes from that plant. It takes time. It takes effort. It costs money.

Sewing garments, or hot-gluing costumes is another way for a child to come to grips with how clothing "appears." Maybe you have a closely located relative or friend who likes to sew. Often making a costume can lead to a discussion of the work involved and why it should cost money.

Children who have hands-on experience with how things come into their house are not prone to belief that a god is responsible for those items. Children who are allowed to work for money in the home are not interested in discussions about how "God makes it possible for us to have jobs and buy things." They are immune to the message that good things come from gods. No, they saw it grow. No god popped down and made it appear.

It is also important for children to be involved in the mechanics of health and sickness. Gods do not make one healthy. Devils do not make one sick. Grandma smoked and got lung cancer. I saw a picture of her lungs and heard her wheezing for years. It had nothing to do with her lack of faith or some god deciding to take her to Heaven.

Children who are not pressured by a parent's ideas about clothing will not be prone to pressure from their peers about clothing. Children who are not pressured by their parents' ideas about values will not be prone to pressure from others about their values. Let them have responsibility and they will assume responsibility.

Chapter Sixteen

Crime and Punishment

One of the greatest concerns for a child is abuse and crime outside of the home. The church seeks to cover this in offering their own schools and a rigid standard of values by which children who do wrong can be punished.

This is one of the great hypocrisies of the institutions that claim to "protect" children. There is nothing to prevent religious children from turning on each other any more than there is some kind of reason to who is caught and who is punished. Values are determined by some kind of vague group pressure of the decade – this decade it is antiviolence – and rules are enforced almost at whim. When children go to school it is important for them to understand that justice and fairness are separate matters, that crime and punishment are not always rational, and that there is no appeal to a higher court.

I know many men who were subjected to playground persecution who wished that they had watched *The Godfather* at an early age. Stories that men tell of wishing that they had not learned restraint from their mothers and teachers and had just gone berserk the first time they were attacked are common and sad. These days a child will be hauled in for any sign of violence whether it was just or not.

Women are taught in self-defense classes to use any power or feeling they have to turn on a male attacker. Boys are not instructed in how to defend themselves, but told that they are bad if they want to defend themselves.

Let us not pretend. Humans are primates. There are alpha-males and the females are alphas while they have babies. Religion claims to have the monopoly on controlling the animal in us, but most times they just make it impossible for the animal to be recognized until it is too late.

"Turn the other cheek" is as realistic for a child as "lie down and whimper." The gestures of submission are not always effective and the appeals to the "higher qualities" often aggravate the fight.

Children should be taught that all humans are capable of acting rationally but that they also can act in an instinctual way. They should be taught that stress brings out aberrant and violent behavior in humans just as it does in rats. Sometimes a demonstration will help a child to understand stress reactions. Toddlers test their mothers to find the points of stress. Kids will test each other when they first find themselves in a group to find the points of stress and determine the differences and weaknesses in other children. No rules will prevent this. It is a group stress procedure.

Christians and New Agers will go on and on about how they have trained the violence out of their children. If you can, start harassing these parents. Call them names, pick at them, use any tactic short of what is illegal to back them into a corner. When they crack – and they will crack – accuse them of not being able to practice what they preach. When they get angry, hold up your hands and tell them that you wanted to show them the difference between imagining how one will act and understanding how one will act under pressure.

If they don't see the point, tell them that their kids are under pressure and that they will act in aberrant and unacceptable ways because of that and the lessons they have learned about love and tolerance will be cast down. The accusations will probably continue to fly because Christians believe that anger and violence is a face of the Devil and to accuse their children of violence is condemning them to Hell.

Explain that they are already in Hell. They are in Hell and dragging your kids into Hell with them.

There are no rational ways out of the playground battle. There are some solutions. You can interfere. You can remove your child. You can have your child try some tactics.

You can stand aside and hope that your children will learn to defend themselves or grow out of it.

I love it when parents say, "Well, Johnny, you must have done something to make them hate you."

Usually the teacher was the one who singled Johnny out. She pointed out that Johnny was new and made him stand up and say something so he looked like a dork. She might have praised him in front of the class. She might have told him he was stupid or implied that he was in someway inferior. Teachers are still under this misconception that children like attention in class. Children like to be called on when everyone else is being called on. They like to be part of the popular circle and the winning team. When no one else knows the answer and Johnny finally gets it, and the teacher praises Johnny and wonders why the rest of the class didn't get it, Johnny is doomed.

If the teacher has some religious notion and Johnny calls her on it and she denounces him, Johnny is doomed. If a popular child has a notion and Johnny disputes it and the group fears for the stability of their hierarchy, Johnny is doomed. If Johnny looks different and the teacher points it out and tells everyone to be tolerant, Johnny is doomed. If the teacher starts the sing-song chant of some religious mantra and the children join in but Johnny doesn't want to or doesn't know the words, Johnny is doomed.

Johnny can sneer at the teacher with some kind of twisted humor and he will win respect from the class but be punished by the teacher. If Johnny demonstrates secret or taboo knowledge and keeps it from the teacher, Johnny will be respected and, again, punished. If Johnny wallops the alpha-boy in a big schoolyard fight, he will be respected and, again, punished. If Johnny thinks up some awful name to call the alpha-boy, he will, again, be respected – and punished.

Johnny (or Susie) needs wits, guts, and stubbornness to survive the schoolyard. But they will need wits, guts, and stubbornness to survive life. Reassure children who are suffering this battle that it is not going to be all that they will get from school. Teach them to be creative about getting in and out of scrapes and jams. The fear and paralysis reaction works among wolves, rarely among humans.

Remember that Christian and New Age kids have probably already learned to lie and pretend that they are innocent and good. Their survival depends on their ability to avoid manipulation and the omniscience of the church, through cheating and being immune to argument and threat of punishment. They have learned to be callous and self-righteous and interested in blaming others for their faults. They have no experience with anyone assuming responsibility for actions. All the evil that they can enjoy is merely temptation by the devil, for which they can be forgiven.

Murder can be forgiven. Why not any of the lesser sins? The religious lesson of hypocrisy is clear in the playground. Morality enforced from outside can be manipulated through lying, and playing along.

"Why would people believe in a god," Craig asked me at the age of seven.

"Because they think that without a god people would be amoral. They think that a god can tell people how to behave," I explained.

Craig nodded. He already had learned about decision and consequence.

"When we don't have a god, it is up to us to take responsibility for our own actions and to make the world a better place."

"Yeah!" he said brightly. "If people act bad then everyone is unhappy and if people act good then everyone is happy!"

"Yes," I replied. "When we give up gods, it is up to us."

Part Three:

Why Am I?

The Adolescent

Chapter Seventeen

The Price of Independence

The final category of personality is one that shows up earlier but becomes a battleground when the stakes get higher in Middle School and High School. You know by now that your child is Extroverted or Introverted, Inductive or Deductive, Object-oriented or Situation-oriented, and now you will see that there are two extremes in dealing with time management.

The religions of the world have the flavor of these two extremes. This is the easiest trait to identify. It is the trait that usually determines, not whether people can get along or not, but whether or not they can live and work together.

One extreme is called *Judging* (J-types) by the MBTI and the other is called *Perceiving* (P-types). Again, I think these are loaded terms. One extreme is the person who times in a linear way and sees time as compartmentalized and sectioned with projects being planned, scheduled, and completed, one at a time. Usually this trickles over into their lives where they prefer things organized and neat. Even their appearance tends to be organized and neat. Efficiency is valued as well as the ability to get the job done. This is Western time, taken to extreme by the Germans, the Calvinists, the Swiss, and the Jews. It is also common to the Japanese, Dutch and Nordic peoples, and Americans. Time is a commodity of value and life is seen to be too short to waste.

The other extreme is the person who times in a circular way and sees time as fluid, non-definable, broad, and abundant. This person will have many projects going all at once and be reluctant to tie any up because there might be a revision or another thought to be added. They wander into meetings late and have to spend a lot of time wandering into the topic of the meeting, if there is one. Flexibility and spontaneity are valued and rigidity is perceived as a weakness. The quest for perfection is valued way more than the time it will take. Their lives are loose, with meals eaten whenever and social events happening on a whim and ending maybe when everyone goes to sleep on the floor. This is Eastern Time, taken to extreme by South Sea Islanders, Hunter-Gatherers, and New Agers. Catholics, Irish, and French, as well as other cultures born in a mild climate, tend toward this kind of time.

In the US this trait is equally divided among the populace along a few cultural, gender, or genetic lines. Like the other traits, being a linear time person in a circular time family will tend to make you less fanatic about it, but, as a teenager, it may become a point of rebellion. Generations tend to show preference for one or the other extreme every twenty years or so. The twenties were loose, the forties were disciplined, the sixties were loose, the eighties were disciplined. Even the drugs of each era are diagnostic: coke and caffeine versus pot and alcohol.

The religious try to make their particular sense of time a part of their code of ethics. Sit around and bliss out on contemplation of the spiral of life versus cleanliness is next to godliness. The Catholics get to pay to get into heaven, the Protestants have to work for it. Being a good Christian is seen as a stamp of approval on a positive work ethic. California is the evil place where everyone sits around in the sun, lives off of welfare, blisses out on pot and watches for UFOs.

If you are going to fight with a teenager in your house it is usually going to be over conflicting time styles. School is not designed for P-people. They will drag to school, drag through their homework, turn everything in late and half-done, and generally irritate everyone around them who wants them to be disciplined. They are weak to the call of meditation and removal from the rat race and will join up to a New Age cult because "they're mellow, dude."

J-children in a P-house will long for order in a chaotic universe where meals are never more than everyone scrambling for whatever and sandwiches get left over from a month ago buried on the coffee table with a lot of newspapers that haven't been read and will probably never get read. This child is vulnerable to the call of order and discipline, of asceticism and deprivation, and punishment for excess. This child may join a fundamentalist church with strict rules and a clear duty roster.

Wall off your house if you need to. Give your children the space to learn to understand their sense of time and accomplishment. Let the P-child wander around Europe for a season. Let the J-child schedule events after school to use time more wisely. Let both children have their own rooms and a section of the kitchen if their preference is different from yours.

The Js in Karen's family think she lives like a hippie. She has no furniture and meals are *ad hoc*. She keeps the housekeeping to a minimum by not having any stuff, but there are always books and projects spread out on the floors. They sleep at odd hours and no one goes to a regular job. Yet, her household pulls in over 100K a year – although they have no savings and no assets and nothing to show for it except memories from all their trips to Europe. Her son thinks this is normal. His values tend toward learning and improving the mind and having as much fun as he can. He is criticized for dressing sloppily and being unconcerned with schedules.

Elizabeth cleans her house sometimes three times a day. Her children have their table in the kitchen and the adult table is permissible only if they can keep their food on their plates. Meals are planned a month ahead of time and bedtime is rigidly enforced. The kids have full schedules and everything is coordinated with precision and punctuality. They make good incomes, have bought a house, pay their bills on time and are investing in mutual funds for retirement and college. Her kids change their clothing five times a day and no one is allowed to use a towel more than once. Elizabeth does fifteen loads of laundry a week. Her children are praised for being neat and well-dressed.

Should you find yourself at odds with a child or a well-meaning relative or a teacher, it may be over time style. Happiness and dissatisfaction often are at flashpoint over this trait in personality. Religion is often offered by one parent as proof to the child that the other parent is "missing out" on something mysterious and interesting. Making an effort to extend the hand of tolerance is often a way to keep a religion from getting hold of your child because of a conflict over lifestyle. Again, be honest. Take responsibility for your own hangups either way, and try creatively to work to make a space for the child in your home so he or she won't have to leave home to find peace.

Here are some ideas:

Ps need space and time. Projects need to be out in the open. What looks cluttered is often an order that is not your order. Thomas Dolby sang a song where the lyric was: "She's gone and tidied up and I can't find anything!" Ps need to goof off and not have things scheduled. This makes them feel trapped. They need classes where there is no homework due and no papers to write on deadline. Tests are okay and they often enjoy "pop" quizzes. They will soak things in rather than seem to study. A P slumped in a chair may actually be thinking about several different things, and the TV is just a way to help with the thought. My father, a P, needs the radio and the TV on – sometimes playing different stations. His house looks like a tornado came through. He lives on cigarettes and coffee and does not seem to eat.

Close the door on a P's room. Just close the door if you can. Close your eyes when they finally go to school in the morning. Ignore the tardy slips. Ask teachers to allow some way to compensate for disruptions – maybe arrange some extra credit. In high school perhaps class loads can be lightened and more time allowed to graduate. Give Ps a refrigerator or a section in the refrigerator with a buffet of sorts. They will never know what they want to eat when. Don't be hurt when they go through the milk one week and let it go bad the next. Get them to see that religion does not offer them the freedom that they require. If you have to, tell

94

them that the search for meaning in life goes on all through life and does not have to be learned at any particular time or in any particular order. They will understand this and think that you are "cool." Don't let Js clean up after you. Firmly tell them that this is your style and give them the kitchen, keeping a shelf for your own whatevers. Js will be miserable trying to organize you. Let the Js organize themselves and draw the line there. Encourage them to set up their own schedules and adhere to their own requirements. Tell them that it's okay to color-coordinate the sock drawer, but don't do your laundry. Give them their own bath if you can. If you can't, try to keep down on dirt in the bathroom. Keep your own mess to your own rooms and try to give common areas a little bit of help. Js will feel frantic if schedules are broken and everyone is late. Calm them down and explain that you will try to be considerate of their schedules if they will be considerate of your slower pace.

Explain to Js that all work and no play is not a reason to work oneself to death. Let them fill the weekend with useful tasks such as classes at the local college or work at a job instead of getting sucked into the idea that the Sabbath is a day that should be filled with religious events. Don't try to organize events if you are an extreme P. Scorn of your inability to do the most common logistical things will further alienate you from Js. Ask instead that they do the organizing and let you sit back and admire their skill.

You should be aware that this preference does not become a blend of traits on the median between the extreme Judger and the extreme Perceiver, making the person appear to prefer some compromise between the two. It becomes spotty. Some will be anal at work and slobs at home. Their socks will be organized and their car will reek with cigarette butts. The midline here is as difficult as the extremes. "No! Don't cut it diagonally!" "What shirt, I don't see any shirt on the floor." "You'd better not be late!" "What homework, oh, yeah, I forgot."

Living in the Light

The "Odd Couple" is a good image of this kind of conflict. Let it stay where it belongs – on the level of where the
toothpaste gets placed and how it is squeezed. If it turns
religious, try to separate cleanliness from godliness before
your child's brain gets washed as well.

Chapter Eighteen

The Crusades

While most Atheists focus on the battle over information, the agonies of families most often come in the teenage years. The Christians are notorious for being able to sense out the vulnerabilities of adolescence and pounce on needy teens. Every year, families are flattened by the suicide of a bright and seemingly well-adjusted teen.

This is where Atheists are at their weakest. The position of being on the defense makes them seem like rabid dogs crying out for more study of paleontology in middle schools. The battle at this level should not devolve into details. Teens lose confidence in people who cannot focus on the issues and constantly hark back to the form of the argument and not the substance. The ground here is BIG. The issues are not over what is learned or why gods don't exist. Any Atheist spending time in arguments with teens or religionists on the issue ground discussing the logical reasons why gods can't exist is helping out religion.

Yes! I said, "helping out religion."

So imagine the ground. The teen is in the middle. The Atheist is on one side and the godmonger is on the other. The Atheist starts going on about the existence of gods and the religionist just smiles. "Can you *prove* that God doesn't exist?" he finally says, still smiling like a snake over a rat. And the rat is hypnotized by that snake's eyes and goes for the argument, completely oblivious that the teen is disgusted and embarrassed.

No, no, and no! If you value this teen, even if the discussion is not in real time, face to face with the deist, never fall for this trap. The discussion is majestic. The discussion is about the fate of the world. It is about war and apocalypse and millions of people being burned alive. The trap is falling from the pinnacle and trying to holler up from the fog about trivia.

Adolescents are awake. They are aware, maybe for the first time, that they are alive and that they are mortal. They have tasted of the fruit of good and evil and are suddenly aware that the issues are MORAL. *All caps.* MORAL. *We* are responsible for mankind. *We* are guilty for the state of the world. *We* have sinned the great sin and our children are dying for it. Think of Wagner. Think of Brünhilde bursting in after the "Ride of the Valkyries," trying to save humanity. The *Götterdämmerung* is upon us and the battle is not between mortals. Think of Jeanne d'Arc with a sword in her hand blazing into the battle against the English, all of France rising to her call.

Man, you're a lost cause. How can the existence of a god compare to the terror and passion of St. Stephen's body pierced with a hundred arrows? Adolescents' thirst for passion and thrill and drama makes them very, very, very vulnerable to the most extreme factors in religion. Girls become nuns. Boys go out and pump lead into the infidel Jews who stole their ancestor's lands. Girls run away to follow someone like Reverend Jim Jones as though he were a rock star. Adolescents know that you will laugh at them. Their passions become secret. Like Victorian romances, the taboo of passion flames in their hearts and makes those forbidden meetings with that cult like a balm on a fiery soul.

Most adolescents wear out their passions in cars and football and lusting after the unobtainable queen or king of the homecoming. But if your house has valued the religious battle over all these years then "beware the Ides of March, Caesar." Don't believe me? Watch *Jesus Christ, Superstar* with your child and see if they fall into the drama of it.

So, what to do? What do you do when you've killed all the gods and no one is on your side to fight the Titans? There is a simple solution, actually. It's been time tested. Every time one country conquers another, the gods of the vanquished turn into devils if they're not transformed or added to the pantheon.

So get on your robes and take up your staff and get onto that box and start up that dramatic, melodious, hypnotic voice and damn the gods to hell where they belong. Disgusting? Get angry. Yes, get angry over all the people who have been murdered and tortured and starved because of religion. They give St. Stephen, you give them back the Children's Crusade. They parade around Jeanne d'Arc, you give them the witch hunters who had her burned. Let your child watch the horror of religion in movies like *Cabeza de Vaca* or *The Mission*.

When people start shoving the drama of passion at your children, don't be cool and logical. Fight back. I don't mean quietly argue, I mean *fight*. Get outraged that they would dare try to rip childrens' minds away and torture them with pain and loss that will be with them all his life. Treat an attack at a teen as if your daughter were going to be raped. But don't be rabid. Be strong and firm and disgusted.

Jesus Christ Superstar is a good place to start. Sure, it's about Jesus, but not about Medieval Jesus or Reformed Jesus, but about Modern Jesus. This portrayal of Jesus is attractive because it is a portrayal of modern man. All the characters are immediately sympathetic to the young audience. The songs are powerful, evocative and sincere. The drama is poignant and realistic. The bad guys are people you would meet on the street and Jesus is not quite sure of himself.

Before you get too angry, look at the pathology. The deists spend a lot of time looking at you and expect you to argue about creation and the nature of their god and not to look too closely at them. Let's take a look at this passionate, modern, attractive story.

It opens with Judas wondering about the wisdom of Jesus and agonizing over Jesus passing up opportunities to help the world. He is angry and frustrated and lost in the desert. This clues us in. Judas is everyman. Judas is every kid in the audience who is now hooked. "My mind is clearer now. At last, all too well, I can see where we all soon will be. If you strip away, the myth from the man, you will see where we all soon will be." What concerned adolescent can resist the pathos in this concern?

Then the apostles are all drunk and unconcerned and Jesus is trying to get them aroused. Is this not the teen trying to get his world to get interested in the real problems he sees around him? Then Mary tries to soothe him and she is condemned for being a whore. Then we flash to all the bad guys concerned about this man who is causing trouble. Caiaphas is deliciously evil with a bass rumble "we need him crucified." He is the head of authority. He is the established, corrupted church. The teen delights that Jesus defies him. And then we are shown the fame of Jesus through the figure of Simon the Zealot. Simon cried out for Jesus to used his fame for glory and the overthrow of Rome. But we have just seen that Rome is not the enemy, the enemy is the dark face of the conspiracy to have Jesus put to death. Jesus is tormented by the sick who are pathetic, yet creepy. He is angry and troubled about his fate, but he cannot blame Judas. Judas is everyman. Judas is confused and tormented and hangs himself.

The power of this opera is in the fact that Jesus is pushed around and kicked and beaten and resigned. The teen feels this way. Walled in and persecuted. Wanting Justice and receiving lies and jokes. Pontius Pilate is one of the most sympathetic villains in the history of movie making. He is the hand of the one man who can make a difference, that one teacher. But Jesus is sullen by now and unreceptive. Pilate is tormented, yet cannot fight the will of the people.

The introduction of Pilate into this movie in such a big way is telling. It shows the child that good people cannot fight the will of the masses. Pilate symbolizes the adult who is faced with forces beyond his control. Children see that they will become Pilate if they try to work within the system. Jesus is given a way out, but he turns it down. His own friends then turn against him. He is alone.

Who can resist this man alone? This man who has no more strength to fight the evil of the world? We are drawn in by Judas's anger and now are hoping, hoping for this "sad and lonely man." This man is killed and Judas screams out in anger from "Heaven." This is no longer a story about a martyr, it is a story about a rebel, a persecuted man who wanted to change the world.

When this opera first hit broadway, the Christians went wild in denouncing it. It has stood the test of time. It gives the teen a voice, "My God, my God, why have you forsaken me? ... Take this cup away from me, for I don't want to taste its poison. Feel it burn me, I have changed, I'm not as sure as when we started. Then I was inspired, now I'm sad and tired. . ."

As a parent, you must understand that the story is universal. The story is the story of every single man who ever felt alone, betrayed, and unsure. As an Atheist, you need to separate the story from the trappings of religion. As a parent, you need to give the story to your children and teach them that the story is there even when religion is not.

Chapter Nineteen

Arriving at the Source

At some point in adolescence, some children become fascinated with theory. "Why do things work?", becomes more important than the "how do they work?" of the earlier years. When a child wants a discussion on theory, then you can pull out the "proving that a god exists" hat and get ready to reveal the "man behind the curtain."

Proof

In approaching the question of the existence of gods, I take the historical approach. Take the Bible and let the child read the great books out there that prove that the stories were all paraphrased from other places, translated with a slant toward the times, and filled with mess-ups like the word "spirit" to mean "ghost." Start a discussion or an investigation into semantics and the intricacies of translation. Offer the histories of other religions and let the child understand how religion is a reflection of culture. Go into the history of religion. Give accounts of bogus miracles and witch hunts, pogroms of one religion against another because of stupid reasons like a king owing too much money for a war.

This can be quite effective, as the following testimony shows:

I was one of those Christians who believed that women who got abortions should suffer the death penalty. My brother, an Atheist, was very patient with me and did not harass me for my fanaticism, but I could not help feeling that it was so sad that he had turned from the church and was doomed to hell.

I became curious with reading about the "real" Jesus. I started to read documents written by other people about the ancient Christians. Gradually, I grew more and more horrified with the persecution and animosity of these Christians and I realized that the Church had not changed. I have since denounced my church and become an agnostic.

There May Be Wheat in the Chaff

Let the child understand that wisdom is often independent from belief. A person can make some brilliant observations about human nature and couch them in religious or mythological or mystical terms. Explain that even the best philosophers and scientists often have a mystical side. One must separate the wheat from the chaff when one starts learning history and theory.

When teens are interested in philosophy and psychology and understand that there are brilliant observations sometimes obscured in strange language, they can look for the truth without being distracted by the decoration. Often, a teen, (or an adult) will be drawn into the esoteric face of religion and find some fascinating truths there about the nature of perception, human fallibility, and understanding and practicing the arrival at "enlightened" mental states. The studies of Gnosticism (Christian), Cabalism (Jewish), Sufism (Moslem), Yoga, and Zen are all attractive disciplines and are filled with brilliant people doing brilliant (and inspirational) work. They are very, very different from the fundamentalist or traditional sides of religion and acknowledge themselves to be the place where people move when religion no longer satisfies their questions. Most of the people I know who study these disciplines often have IQs of over 120, are professors or very well read, are extremely tolerant, rational, and down-to-earth. Children introduced to these studies will think that they have found the real source and be furious when you try to attack.

A better way is pointed out by one of my recent correspondents:

> Over the years, I understood that the wisdom of the esoteric studies was universal. I began to try to search for a "reality" to the wisdom I have found in these studies. I decided eventually that to take up the mantle of any religion was to hide myself from the truth that

might lie in that religion. When my Sufi friends would begin to discuss Sufism, I would be welcomed into the discussions, but when pressed, I would say, "I must remain without a crutch when I am faced with the emptiness of contemplating the infinite." I think that the discipline of holding that fear and resisting the temptation to reach for an easy answer is more important for me than accepting the comfort of Allah." My friends were extremely respectful of this and I found that dervishes and teachers were also respectful of this position. It allowed me an inside track from where I could watch and remain an unbeliever.

Checking the Source

One of the ways to critique and uncover contradictions in religion is to trace the philosophy back to a source and to place a work in historical and social context. Offer contemporary works as a way to judge whether a work was considered bogus by rational people or heretical by dogma-bound people or fanciful or earth-shattering. Give some idea of how the process of acceptance of a theory works.

Also teach a child to severely judge accepted theories in the sciences and technology. Christopher Columbus was not the only person who thought the world was round. The other people who knew it to be round also knew from accurate measurements that it was much larger than Columbus thought. The Dark Ages were confined only to Continental Europe. Ireland was practicing medicine and had plumbing when England was being eaten alive by plagues and dirt. And cosmology is based on three tiny observations which can readily be dismissed and the whole theory of the big bang may be nothing but a guess.

Consider the following experience:

My father made a religion out of science. Everything scientists said was true and everything non-scientists said was criticized. He trusted the rigor of the scientific method to weed out the irrational out of science. The reason I say that it was a religion for him, is that when I got my degree from MIT in physics I was introduced to the grad program and discovered that there were hundreds of bogus theories that were being funded. People that I should have respected were so full of arrogance and pride over their pet theories that they would attack and condemn anyone who wanted to do contradictory research.

I discovered that research was more dependent upon one's political position in the university than in the nature of the work. Over and over again, I saw scientists get browbeat out of departments, go somewhere else to work, do some brilliant work to disprove the accepted theory and still be condemned by the established community. They were mavericks and not to be trusted. I became so sickened by these attitudes that I left the university and did not finish my degree. I now have to rely on private funding for my research.

Question Everything

Knowledge *should* fall prey to criticism. Otherwise it is dogma. If you persist in some "belief" that seems scientific you undermine your credibility. The first good thing you can tell your child is "I don't know."

Where did the "fact" come from? How many people made the same observation independently? What about the equipment needed to observe the fact? How many people can duplicate the machinery? Who stands to lose if the fact is disproved?

There are some "out-there" fields of study that deserve study from a historical point of view just to reveal the conservative nature of science and how science is not immune to beliefs and priesthoods. The study of midwifery reveals the dogmatic nature of the AMA and the limitations of the profession of medicine in helping the healthy as well as curing the sick. The study of spaceflight reveals the difficulty and expense of trying to maintain a monolithic science run by one agency. The study of psychology reveals the problems involved in separating out real statistics from unrealistic sample size and shows how a profession can be clouded from one direction by the occult and from the other direction by good-old-boy medicine.

Introduce the study of statistics, error margin, sample sizes and random sampling. Introduce the study of journalism and "eyewitness" accounts. The play *Twelve Angry Men* shows the fallibility of the eyewitness. The study of optical illusion and magic demonstrates the art of fooling the senses.

The Map is Not the Territory

The fault of so many, many scientists and others who do excellent work in one field is that they compartmentalize the knowledge. They do not take the lessons learned from one topic, generalize the lesson, and apply it to everything else that moves. Modern religion depends on the compartmentalizing of criticism. You use this part of your brain for science and this part of your brain for "squishy stuff" like religion, ethics, child rearing, or interacting with your girlfriend.

The other extreme that one often sees is taking a "map" from one discipline and filtering the entire world with it. This is common when a brilliant cosmologist tries to talk about the brain, or when an engineer tries to talk about economics. Blatant mistakes are made, the scientist's "real" work becomes suspect – all because of insistence on using one country's map to navigate another country.

Humans are map makers. They have to see reality through some filter in order to generalize and understand connections and to do pattern recognition. One of the things that should be part of the scientific method is to question the map if the data will not fit very well. Making data fit the map is a gross error.

Teach your child that no question is stupid. No subject is too simple. All should fall before the knife of skepticism. If any part of life remains a sacred cow – even stupid things like how to drink water, or which sock to pull on first – then the mind begins to atrophy. Explain that it is like exercising your feet and forgetting to exercise your arms. Your life will also be prey to scrutiny. Be prepared to look at it before you defensively accuse children to mind their own business or save the questions for school.

Expect some curiosity about religion and don't go frothing at the mouth at a request to read the Bible or a visit to a church. Be confident of the tools that children have. Their own experience will mean that they want to see for themselves rather than rely on what you have said. Check it out. See for yourself. Then discuss what was seen and why it was unreal and untenable and just a "bunch of ballyhoo."

Chapter Twenty

Suicide and Other Death-Defying Acts

There is no good research explaining why some children wake up suddenly at twelve and take all the troubles of the world on their shoulders and why some don't pay attention to much of anything until their late thirties. There is some suggestion that extremes of personality may have a correlation with intelligence in teens and their susceptibility to idealism, fanaticism, and rebelliousness.

Parents seem to think that if their teenagers could be locked up and sedated they might fare better. Although challenging, the teen years may be the best for some parents. Many teens wake up to adult issues and show deep concern for the state of the world around them. Another mixed reaction in teens is the reaction to death. Youth seems to react in several ways.

Fascination with suicide is a common response to a growing awareness of mortality. Often teens feel that if death is random then taking their lives is a way to take control. If a god is offered to this kind of teen as a kind of control, the teen will be vulnerable to this message. The real solution to this situation is change. Death is a metaphor for change in many cultures that have heavy-handed initiation rituals. Sending a teen on a trip of personal significance, changing schools, jumping into college early, even permitting a radical change of outward appearance can give a sense of control back into a life stagnating or going haywire. The following is a recounting by Sandra, a smart girl who had trouble as far back as grade school.

For me, life had a cutting edge to it. I craved to live on that edge and to never fall into the sleepy world around me. By the time I was fourteen, I realized that I was the kind of person who did well in a war but not well in a time of peace. I hungered for issues and triumphs and the rich language of the books I loved where the heroine was in a foreign land, doing something meaningful and exciting.

I was not the kind of person who could fantasize. I was not content to read and hope for a future where I might save the world. I wanted it with a hunger that overrode any of the concerns around me. I had a great loneliness to talk to someone about things that meant something. I knew at twelve that I was trapped in a world that was foreign to me, separated from a world which I could see and taste and feel, but which did not exist.

Death was the only thing which frightened people around me. Death was taboo. Death was a possibility. Death was associated with important things. Playing with death made me feel as though I could exit my trap. I was curious about death. At thirteen I understood that I had to reject faith in an afterlife because I would become too curious to remain alive. Death also was a kind of peace from the passions that I felt and could not express.

After my fifth suicide attempt, I realized that I sought a drama of death. I then tried to plan a death that would have a long drama attached to it. For the month leading up to my seventeenth birthday, I would focus on my death. For the first two weeks I wore all black and covered my arms and my hair as if in mourning. The next week I wore all gray and the final week, I wore all white still covering my head and arms. I planned a birthday party but also planned my suicide. The expectations of the people I invited to the party added a kind of flavor to the fact that I would die before that party or change myself into something so different as to be like being reborn. As the date approached, I realized that what I wanted at that moment was a dramatic change like death. Then I realized that my awareness was so sharpened by the threat of death until each moment was glorious and one more moment I was truly alive. The fact of my coming death made me view my acquaintances as if my time with them were limited and they became more dear to me.

I discovered so many valuable things in this elaborate scheme of death that by the time the day arrived and I wore color and let my hair down, I felt so changed that I felt that I should not recognize the person that I was.

Yet, I had not been able to talk to anyone about my experience before or after my "transformation" for I changed my mind about wanting to die by the time the day arrived. I understood that there was something very valuable around the subject of death, yet no one could talk about it. Later when I read about the Japanese ceremony of ritual suicide and the varied initiation ceremonies around the world involving a kind of death, I felt cheated by my culture. So many times I had wanted to die, and the fear that people had of death kept me from understanding that it was not bad or sick or foolish to long for a radical change like death, but a very important aspect of humanity that can add dimensions to a flat life.

Another reaction is senseless abandon, often in a group. If the teen is extroverted or emotional, getting lost in a group that is flirting with strong flights of emotion is a release and an addiction. The strong pull of cults and lay witness missions lies in their ability to give shared emotional release. Do not underestimate the power of throwing oneself into the snake dance or the power of driving screaming drunk with your buddies at three in the morning. A death can cause such persons to go into a mode wherethey challenge death and try to prove that they are alive again and again. It is often the result of a teen's feeling numb or unable to feel. This child is extremely vulnerable to the tie of religion.

It used to be acknowledged in long-lasting wakes that death brought out a kind of fury and gluttony in some people. Even the knowledge of death or a fear of aging can bring out this kind of reaction. There are not many safe outlets, but giving children something dangerous may be frightening in the short term yet protect them from seeking release through religion. Sports offer the best outlet for an active, expressive child. Drama and the stage can also be an outlet that is safe for the overactive imagination.

During the teenage years, flirtation with danger and shared emotional release may be extreme:

> When I was in high school, the thing we did was to get drunk out of our minds and then ride down to the train tracks. There, we would wait for the trains and try to jump the slower moving freights. We knew it was dangerous, but maybe we didn't care. I don't know. The point of getting drunk is so you don't care.

Living in the Light

My parents were run-of-the-mill. My Dad was always harping on being a good Christian, to stop hanging out with a "bad" crowd and getting my grades up for college. Huh! If he could have seen inside my mind and known that I thought of college as one more door to slam on the jail of my life. Like I really wanted to cram for tests for the next five years! Church and grades. But I knew that there was no escaping it. It was like a train bearing down on me. Maybe jumping trains was a way to say "screw you!" to my father and his endless expectations and responsibilities. I wanted to have fun while I was young enough to enjoy it.

It was the three-thirty train that did us in. Most of us had jumped in the car. Carrie kept running but she was so drunk that she kept stumbling. I grabbed her finally and, I don't know, I guess she slipped. The train wheel cut both her feet off. Well, I got my responsibility and I got my hell. But unlike my father, Carrie never blamed me. She was so incredible. She learned to walk on fake feet, you know. Like nothing ever happened. I tried to go to her in the hospital and take the blame, but she wouldn't let me. She showed me what real courage is and real responsibility. She also showed me that life is not hanging out with the wrong crowd, but that in any crowd there are those people who are real heroes.

Another reaction to death that leads a child to the wide lap of religion is the senselessness of the world. Why me? Give me a reason! Religions jump at this call and give solace, comfort and the pap of purpose in the universe. Often this child rejects the rational argument and wants the security of a personal kind of universe. The way out for teens is to give them something to make or to grow or to care for. Gardens are extremely good for the teen who cannot come to grips with the roulette wheel of the world. A garden shows the effects of neglect, poor planning, weather, and yet, blooms and grows in the face of the odds. Tending something is a way to turn the tables on the security of religion, offering would-be "victims" the opportunity to be their own gods.

Rational teens who lock themselves away from their emotions are another target for religion when a crisis like death occurs. This kind of person compartmentalizes life and relegates the mystery of death and the unknown to religion – even while knowing that it is irrational. Such persons half listen to the "pap" but are comforted by the ritual and formality of the traditional model. They often have no time to think about alternatives or "squishy" issues. When crises occur, they grab at something near, unprepared and frightened by the task of thinking about untenable matters.

Such teens need the practice of religion divorced of the ideology of religion. Give these teens the idea of having a place to meditate or a place where they can allow themselves to feel — a shrine without shrine-ness, so to speak. Give them a compartment in which to put grief, loss, and fear of the unknown. Often these teens can respond favorably to going away to the mountains or the sea to think and be in the world. But they need a pre-established place and routine so they aren't flailing around when the crisis comes.

The following account is typical of how this personality type reacts to death:

My mother died when I was sixteen. Man, there is nothing, *nothing* in my world that prepared me for that. I just wanted to curl up and die. All I could think about was the senseless of her being killed like that. I couldn't think. I couldn't eat. I had always loved science, but now, when I tried to go back to my books, I could only see her face teaching me about electricity and multiplication. She never laughed at my wanting to be a chemist. My father wanted me to be a football player. Now I felt like I had let him down and her memory was going to make it impossible for me to live my dreams.

My cousin Effy got me to go to Temple. She got me to say the words and go through the Jewish ritual of mourning. It's really neat. You get together and talk about the dead person. No one ever talked to me about my Mom. I think they were all afraid to say anything. I found that I could concentrate on my studies in the day and go talk to people and pray at night. It got me through that horrible time. I guess everyone needs religion for when times get bad.

The kinds of reactions to death are varied and often violent. Religion has had a monopoly on death for aeons. It is a place to catch people at their weakest.

Why don't people insure their lives against disaster? As parents, you can teach your children rituals and a way to face death with closure and knowledge that it is a grim fact. The afterlife is a candy-coated pill to still the fear of death. All kinds of cults pop up to offer an afterlife. Among the more outrageous are the new cryonics groups that freeze members' bodies or heads as a "better alternative to death." Yes, that might be so, but there is not as yet any technology that will repair the brain damage done in freezing. Yet, these people, often brilliant scientists and engineers, found that having a membership in a cryonics group freed them from the fear of death with the possibility of an afterlife.

One of my great friends in Junior High used to say, "Anne, when you die you rot." It used to make me angry. And she'd say. "Why can't you face it? When you die you rot." Today, I have decided that to live with the fear of death intact is a good discipline. It is like Joey whose friend got her feet cut off, or Sandra who learned that an awareness of death can make life more acute. But I still have not accepted that we should just lie down and die and pray for an afterlife. I guess I feel that I'm going to go kicking and screaming all the way. Each time we complete another EEG study I say to myself, "that's one more nail in the coffin of death."

Chapter Twenty-One

"For the World is Hollow and I Have Touched the Sky"

Very few parents can prepare their child for disillusion and the violent reactions to dying and growing old.

My favorite teacher in high school was a Viet Nam veteran. He had been a very idealistic young man and had volunteered for the Marines. He was one of the few teachers I ever respected because he admitted to being dead inside from that experience and he warned against idealism as setting oneself up for a fall. I did not think he was right, but I appreciated his candor and the stories that he told of the frustration of that war.

My favorite teacher in junior high school was an Austrian who had gone into the cellar with her family on her tenth birthday and, when they went back up the stairs, she found that their house had been bombed from over their heads. She fell in love with a man at the university and married him not knowing that he was of the royal family of Burma. She escaped Burma with her life and never saw him again during their revolution.

To me, these people were real. They had survived the discovery that the world is not necessarily a nice place. But they did not try to "protect" their students. They did not offer some explanation that some god had wanted to show them something or that the world was evil and that Heaven was the only escape. They were both very matter-of-fact and these events were something that had just happened to them. They were both still wondering about the cruelty and irony of these events, but the events had not made them faithful or dishonest.

Often the only people who talk to children about life-threatening events are those who use the story as a way to push the child into religion. "When I found I was going to die, I turned to God for the first time in my life..." Children are "protected" from the facts of life.

An example of where this can lead:

> My mother gave me a wonderful childhood. My father was abusive and schizophrenic, but I never knew because she was so good at hiding things from me. Life was magical for me as a child. She never told me that my imaginings were not real or that the world was a bad place. She did everything for me because her own childhood had been unpleasant and she thought that children should have happy childhoods.
>
> When I went out into the world, I was completely naïve. I didn't know any bad people were out there. I didn't even know how to survive. I literally went insane. It was too much for me to deal with. I retreated into my world of fantasy and curled up into a ball and ignored all the bad things that happened to me. It took me fifteen years to come to grips with the reality of the world. I don't blame her, she is still a gentle and loving person, but she could have prepared me better.

Religions depend on the young to fall into a mishap and then panic. A bad love affair, a death, an illness or accident, failure to get into the right school, social failure, facing the boredom of the work world, realizing that they are ugly or unacceptable: these are all ways in which the young fall prey to the solace of religion. Ten out of the ten people I spoke with who admitted to taking up a belief even though it was not something they could condone rationally, admitted that the fear of death paralyzed them and the only way they could function was to believe in an afterlife.

There is a wonderful episode of *Star Trek* titled "The World is Hollow and I have Touched the Sky." It shows an old man who has learned this and asserts it even when he is killed by the pain from the "Instrument of Obedience." (By the way, *Star Trek* does many wonderful episodes where religion is exposed.) This phrase is so poignant and true. I used to use it whenever I was faced with some disappointment about the world. The image of this little old man dying just to be able to say this about his world was powerful enough to make me realize that understanding that the world would not live up to my expectations was brave.

Teens need images of people who are brave or have survived the rocky road of the world. Fairy tales are full of images of people who kept on trying even against amazing odds. Movies like *My Left Foot*, a movie about a man who learned to paint and write with his foot, or Helen Keller stories, provide images of people who have come up on the wrong side of the world but ended up accepting the hardship of life with a kind of spirit that makes them attractive for the religious to co-opt.

God is not needed. It is life. It is the spirit, the act of breathing even when death is imminent or pain is all around. What some teens crave to hear is not that there is a reason for bad things happening (punishment of a god) or the story of Jonah, but that badness is not enough to halt the spirit of life, only to slow it down. Children should learn that they can overcome almost any kind of trial of the spirit because that is what the brain *does*. An animal has no way to project backwards or forwards. An animal cannot put things into perspective. An animal cannot see beyond the immediate landscape of pain or handicap to a place where it can win. Humans have such a confidence when they have survived against great odds. The Outward Bound program is designed to give back confidence to teens who are down and out by letting them learn that they can fight nature and win.

This perspective is something teens lack. People in their nineties who are not crippled by pain often have this kind of equanimity about events – the "this, too, shall pass" attitude that is often seen to be religious. But it is not religious. It is perspective. A child will not listen to an adult saying "Oh, yeah I went through that but I survived." No, you did *not* go through "that." Teens need a vision of someone who has gone through something that *feels* like what they are experiencing. The image needs to be life and death or an impossible handicap. If the image is not exaggerated it has no meaning for the teen, because this is the first pain, the first handicap, the first setback. There is no comparison, no way to evaluate the pain next to other pains. This is why some children who have experienced early hardship seem to pass through adolescence with the face of the wise. They have a measure by which to weigh the trials and know that this, too, shall pass.

Religion will supply these images. Look at the fascination with Anne Frank and Jeanne d'Arc. Again, do not tear down the images, but offer your own so that the child can separate bravery and persistence from religion.

Chapter Twenty-Two

Epiphanies and Visions

This is the area in which most rational parents goof up. The current craze against drugs is a way to try to stem the influence of the altered state on the child. When it comes to drugs, many an otherwise rational parent will go berserk.

I have been involved with brain research for many years. Everything is dependent upon the brain. Not the mind, the *brain*. Visions are in the brain. Imagination is in the brain. Ecstasy is in the brain. Hallucinations are in the brain. Moods are in the brain. Nothing, *nothing* is a part of the mind and, therefore, could be dismissed as not being real. If you do this, you will lose this child. If you dismiss a strange event as "just a figment of your imagination," you will be invalidating the child's experience and forcing him or her to think that experience is not as good a guide as once thought. Once the evidence of the senses is invalidated, the child is on the road to religion.

The senses do not lie. A short time ago, any woman who had mood swings was considered to be "hysterical." A little while before that she was "possessed by the Devil." Now we have discovered that PMS can be as mild as suffering from a day of increased irritability to two weeks of uncontrollable hell. Every year new herbs and drugs are discovered to help mitigate the effects of this hormonal swing. Men also suffer from hormone dump. Many men I know vividly recall being quite sane and then experienced an insanity that lasted almost twenty-five years. Once the testosterone levels in their blood drop in the late thirties they feel enormously relieved as if they, again, have control over their brain. I feel sorry for young men. There they are, minding their own business; a young woman walks by and they can no longer think.

These hormonal effects are suppressed in taboos and mystique. Religions seek to use or suppress them. Marriage, celibacy, taking up the veil, polygamy, adultery: they are all effects of people feeling out of control over the effects of hormones.

There is a funny, little-known story about Rachel, the wife of Jacob. Supposedly, she was really the heir of the religious leadership of the tribes which was overlooked in the patriarchal revision that took place later. She was caught in her tent with the idols handed down to her from time unknown when they were doing one of the "round up and destroy all idols" pogroms. She sat on them. Because she was menstruating, she was taboo and no men were allowed to go near her. Another example of people getting around religion by using religion!

Warn upcoming adolescents of the effects of hormones. Young men should understand that their bodies are going to go haywire for a long, long time. Explain that this is evolution at it's finest and give them a copy of *The Selfish Gene* by Richard Dawkins. Explain that they are being used and that to blame women for their feelings or to use women to fulfill their feelings will do nothing to make them go away. Be frank. Tell them that they are going to be uncomfortable or in hell for the next few years but that it gets more manageable as they pass out of their prime. Permit them any way to deal with it that doesn't involve using someone else.

Young women understand all too readily that they go crazy. That's the point. They actually think that they *are* going crazy. They lose confidence in their minds and fall easily prey to the idea that the mind is uncontrollable and unpredictable and not to be relied upon at any cost. PMS warps everything. It is like drinking a hundred cups of coffee mixed with bouts of depression and despair. Isolation from irritants works, so does permitting the young woman to stay in bed all day and not go to school for a day or two out of the month. PMS does not follow genetic guidelines, so a woman who did not suffer may have a daughter who is in hell and agony for two weeks. Lisa's mom dismissed her symptoms with a simple "PMS doesn't run in our family."

Lisa had to ditch her classes and lie, curled up in agony on the floor of the girls' bathroom. She took to alcohol as a muscle relaxant and was an alcoholic by the age of seventeen. Her parents persisted in thinking that she was stupid and irresponsible.

Going without food or sleep will cause hallucinations. Religions advocate fasting and skipping sleep as a way to get closer to their gods. Well, it does the trick all right. A teen who experiences hallucinations is not irrational or trying to get attention. The child who persists in having hallucinations will turn to anyone who will acknowledge and listen to the problem. Religions live off of innocent people who experience hallucinations. Almost every saint and every guru was a victim of hallucinations. Voices, visions, even smells can be hallucinated.

Again, be frank and proactive. Explain to a child that life is full of hallucinations. A new environment, a stressful study period like cramming for exams, dieting, forgetting to eat, not getting enough REM sleep will all lead to massive hallucinations. REM deprivation is the most common cause of hallucinations. Your child should know that REM sleep occurs in small bursts through the night from ten minutes in the first two hours to almost an hour by the time the sleeper has slept more than eight hours. People cannot wake up very well unless they are in REM sleep. Encourage children to pay attention to REM and to try to set their alarms to account for non-REM grogginess. Sleeping in short bursts will cause REM deprivation and victims will grow more and more "insane" until they start hallucinating. But also note that teens need the least sleep of any age. Their bodies are on "high" mode, so don't force them to sleep any more than is healthy.

A "runner's high" is punishing the body to the point where the endorphins must take over. Endorphins are the natural opiates of the body. If runners force themselves into great pain for this "high," you must understand that opiates will make a person feel good. Heroin is universally damned, but the fact exists that it makes a person feel good, really good. Teens will be faced with the fact that something so bad can feel so good and be in a battle between their bodies and their morals.

Addiction is relative. The "fact" that opiates are addictive depends entirely on the addict. Some people report no addiction, some take one hit and are lost forever. Personality and past history are clues to addiction. Again, religions point to gods as a way to fight addiction or as a result of addiction if you live in regions where opiates are a way to connect to the local god. A child who is basically frustrated or unhappy will be more susceptible to addiction. A loner child will be vulnerable. A child who is into experiencing emotional "highs" – adrenaline and endorphins – will be a good candidate for addiction. A bad life full of hopelessness will turn people to the "fix" of opiates.

Opiates are a "down" good feeling; cocaine is an "up" good feeling. Where opiates will attract the loner and the person who seeks comfort and peace, cocaine will attract those who are socially insecure or those who want to be excited and charged and get addicted to the confidence and the fearlessness. If your child longs to be more acceptable or fights mood swings, coke will fill the need.

Marijuana is the most damned drug in the history of drugs, even though it is far less addictive than alcohol or nicotine. Most find that it is not addictive. It has no recorded harmful effects on the body. Pot can be a great way to understand that the mind is a construct of the brain. Religions, on the other hand, seek to throw novices into an altered state to undermine the reliance they have on their minds as instruments to be trusted.

Thus, all meditation is said to discipline the mind, but most teaching requires that the novice empty the mind. Rarely do you see the instruction to focus the mind as when doing calculus problems. Often there is fasting and chanting that accompanies meditation. After an hour of chanting, the mind goes numb and creates visions and altered sensations as if the person were in a sleep-deprivation tank. Other religious ceremonies may involve setting up a path of association wherein the novice can learn hysteria in a safe and meaningful context. Religious ceremonies "work" when some part of the mind is altered – whether it be mood or perception.

Some people report that when getting stoned for the first time they "went insane." It frightened them so much that some were crippled by the experience. Marijuana acts to filter the information from the senses. People find that they are more sensitive to touch and that the world has become a fascinating place. Pot creates a euphoria and sometimes a paranoia. People who find life boring or painful find intense relief with the use of marijuana. It should be understood that this drug is useful in its place and would be wonderful for old people in chronic pain or others who are crippled with the suffering of the world and would appreciate temporary relief without having to rely on some religious "fix." This drug will attract the creative, the loner, the sensate, and those who desire a relief from boredom.

If it were legal, I would almost advocate a teen smoking pot to understand that the mind is a construct of the brain. This would prevent the accidental epiphany that a teen might experience in a religious setting. If one has already "seen god" in a controlled situation or had some revelation due to pot, it will make other religious experiences seem contrived. Meditation can lead the innocent to a whole series of epiphanies that will be misconstrued as due to the meditation or the contemplation of the name of a god.

If you are squeamish about drugs and don't want to break the law, letting children meditate and fast will provide an altered-state experience that will help them understand that the state of the mind is dependent on the state of the brain. Teens are impressionable and will imprint on all the the particulars of an event. They need those particulars to recreate the mental state. A man who has a shoe fetish is in the same state as a teen who became "addicted" to racing around at night on a motorcycle screaming his head off.

Imprinting is good if you need to mate for life and you will meet your wife as a fourteen year old; but as "oldies" stations know, imprinting is big business. Religions use imprinting as a way to create nostalgia and a longing for the particulars of an event that created a moment of an altered state in a teen. Gazing at the cross while listening to the chanting of a group of ecstatic people all of whom are young and attractive may wed a teen to the experience in a way that you will not be able to break.

And so? Create your own market of altered states for the teen. Epiphanies, revelations, visions, "highs," and imprinting are all part of the normal brain. This is so hard for parents to accept. It makes their position weak and the teen vulnerable to these normal occurrences.

We must not, however, forget that altered states and altered behaviors can also be the result of disease processes:

> I had no idea I had developed epilepsy in my fourteenth year. I thought I was going insane. I had the kind of epilepsy that was preceded by a week of intense clarity of thought and sensitivity to light, sound, and touch. Then, rapidly, I would lose my ability to form coherent sentences, become partially paralyzed in my right extremities, suffer from intense sensitivity to light and sound, and finally lose the ability to talk and go into convulsions.
>
> My mother was intensely irritated by this behavior and would yell at me for trying tricks to get out of going to school when she had to pick me up at the nurses' office. I was afraid to tell her that I was insane for fear that they would have me locked up in a loony bin. I enjoyed the intense clarity of mind, but the convulsions I kept secret for fear that I was really sick and my Mom would be mad at me. She was intensely competitive and wanted me to succeed in life. I took these episodes as a fact that I could not measure up to her expectations. It wasn't until I was thirty that I suspected that I might have a "real" disease. I just thought that I went insane every once in a while. I once went to the hospital and they wanted to put me in the crazy ward because the convulsions would eventually go away and I would sleep for 15 hours and be fine. I discovered that I had *petit mal* epilepsy in the left frontal lobe and that all the symptoms from the clarity of mind to the being fine after sleeping for a long time were perfectly normal. Now I can take anticonvulsives and avoid a stroke, but the peace of mind of knowing that what I experienced was real was the biggest relief of my life.

Chapter Twenty-Three

The Missionary

If your son approaches you and announces that his girl-friend invited him to her church, remember that you're going to fight his feelings for this girl. Remove the girl from the battle. Start showing remorse that the girl is a captive of these people. Rationally recite the bloody (they're all bloody) history of this church and ask your son why he has not tried to rescue her. Don't be all against his going to church. If a friend or a lover is the instrument of conversion, let your child be the romantic savior of the maid from the dragon.

Immediately, your son feels that you are on his side. The girl is special. He thinks she's special. If she's special, she deserves the light. She does not deserve to be dragged into death and despair by this insanity. He will look at you with a new light in his eyes. He gets to be the hero and rescue the princess! If you had defamed the girl or the friend, you would have denounced his ability to value and see something in these people. He will have to defend his ability. He will have to go to the church and defend her religion for her. And you have given his head to the church on a silver platter.

At the adolescent level, no one person is bad. Never, never. Only the institution is bad. Adolescents are concerned about fighting dragons. The people in their lives that have faces are valued. The enemy has no face. No officer ever orders a soldier to go kill Bob. You know him, go kill him. Even if he knows Bob, Bob is not Bob. Bob is the enemy. The missionary will show the face of a friend to your child. Never attack the missionaries. Pity them. Extol their virtues and their bravery at trying to make the world a better place. Shake your head at their misdirection and let the child take on the responsibility of extending the hand of truth.

Never resort to details, never attack the individuals. Before Cromwell had to kill half of them, the Irish were invaded from time to time. They looked upon the invaders with a kind of astonishment. Who are you? What's your problem? Oh, you want to live here? No problem. Come join the party, but get washed up first. It became a running joke that everyone that went to Ireland to conquer the Irish became more Irish than the Irish. The same thing happened in Moorish Spain. The Christians would go into the cities all hostile and often end up so much better off that they were disgusted by their own people.

When the missionaries reach out to your child, invite them into the light. Let them see joy and freedom from guilt. Let them see that you do not fear them or their god. Let them see that you care about them enough to want them to be happy. Don't attack their god, but attack that institution with pity and disgust. Let them find out what it means to "wash up" after a lifetime of living in squalor. Not too many people ever reject the light for a life of darkness.

Time after time, entire peoples have been converted due to the charisma, bravery, tolerance, or goodness of an individual missionary. Often missionaries are warned that the opposition will be stiff, the people need to be rescued, and they are being controlled by evil. Friends will feel generous and want to convert the people they love to their religion. Sometimes there is the "Girl Scout cookie" approach going, that the missionary must convert so many people as if it were a sales quota. Often, a person is driven by pride in "saving the little people" from themselves.

A Jehovah's witness can be firmly turned away, but should be told that the reasons for rejection are that the family are all healthy and do not need the drug fix of religion. This invites argument, but maintaining that healthy people do not need to be fixed is better than going into the "existence of god" arguments or the other sales pitches that they are taught to try. You can even explain to them that you know that they are sore-ridden beggar children terrified of defying their mother church and that they envy the healthy and want to see them suffer.

Children will often want to talk to these people. They will be curious as to what they have to say. Forewarn them that these people are sick and think that the cure for their sickness is to believe in spooks. Warn your children that just as beggars will approach them for help to get an alcohol fix, missionaries will approach them to get a spiritual fix. They should also know that all the religious think that other people are suffering from addiction and need a "fix."

A mental teen will be idealistic in crusading for the merits of his or her religion. Your own son may be drawn into this intellectual "fire" and enjoy the arguments. He may find that the woman is attractive and worth fighting. An emotional teen may be passionate in crusading for the values of his religion. Your daughter may find his charisma and passion attractive. The passion may carry over into other aspects of his life, and she will find that it gives her life a kind of rush. She may find that she wants to be near this passion, despite the obvious silliness of the religion.

Children often think they can "sway" loved ones or change them over time. They can put loving pressure on the weaknesses and the broken person will recover over time. Maybe. Often not. You have to bow out here. Telling a teen that this won't work and later saying "I told you so" is being irritating and not very supportive. And you don't know. Some families have flourished on spending a lifetime arguing over issues and fighting over values. It's part of what makes life interesting, the not knowing.

Trust your teens to know that they may have to do something wrong to get something right. Sometimes teens go astray for a few years. If you have successfully conveyed your values to your children and showed them a way to think that will make them question and doubt, one day they may come back and say, "Well, Dad, I guess you were right."

Chapter Twenty-Four

Going to Extremes

It is well known that the more intelligent a teen, the more extreme the personality. The more intelligent the teen, often the more violent the battle for independence. This chapter is a summary of the personality combinations and the points at which you can expect conflict and susceptibility to religion. I will use the MBTI and its vocabulary. Remember that most people show extreme characteristics in only one or two categories. **P-J** (Perceiving-Judging) traits will be on or off for non-extreme types. Conflicts will largely depend on how may traits you do not have in common. **E-I** (Extroverted-Introverted) conflicts are over socializing. **S-N** (Sensing-iNtuiting) conflicts are over methodology and creativity. **F-T** (Feeling-Thinking) conflicts are over getting hurt and pushing for rights. **P-J** conflicts are over lifestyle and time management.

Extroverted or Introverted?

1. Does your child "think" with the mouth? Do you find yourself asking for quiet to let you think?
2. Does your child make friends easily and need to have people around all the time?
3. Does your child seem to be able to study with the radio on or the TV? Does s/he seem to be immune to most information unless it is repeated several times?
4. Does your child have high energy levels and need to be isolated to calm down and rest? Does the child often outwear you, seeming never to stop?
5. Does your child need a lot of interaction and feedback?
6. Does your child get overwhelmed by social events and need time to "detox"?

7. Does your child often prefer to play alone?

8. Does your child resent being told things more than once and seem to remember everything you ever said no matter how irrelevant?

9. Does your child resent interruption, often reacting violently to noise, distraction, or invasion of personal space?

10. Does your child seem to shut down when you think that getting out will help get exposure to new ideas and people?

Descriptors 1-5 indicate Extroversion. Descriptors 6-10 indicate Introversion. A mix indicates no strong preference.

Sensing or iNtuiting?

1. Does your child need to have everything explained in sequence with beginning first and end last?

2. Is your child literal, enjoying body humor more than puns and word plays?

3. Does your child have an amazing memory but no strong attachment to fantasy (no role modeling)?

4. Does your child have to be organized to learn?

5. Does your child need a reason for having something or learning something?

6. Does your child learn at random, with no apparent rhyme or reason to methods employed?

7. Does your child find most people boring and enjoy turning their words and ideas upside down and inside out?

8. Does your child seem to want to reinvent everything from bedtime to the truth?

9. Does your child seem to be a pack rat and need clutter to keep those projects out because there might be something there?

10. Does your child love learning for its own sake and resent having to learn under pressure?

Descriptors 1-5 indicate Sensing. Descriptors 6-10 indicate iNtuiting. Mixed, no strong preference.

Feeling or Thinking?

1. Does your child see the moral side of an issue and want what is fair?
2. Does your child absorb others' problems and take them personally?
3. Does your child seem to intuit others' behavior and have a sense of what others are feeling?
4. Does your child want to help out because it is part of sharing?
5. Does your child need to react strongly and need you to react strongly to play out an emotional drama?
6. Does your child care what is right regardless of how others feel?
7. Does your child seem dense about other people's feelings?
8. Does your child want to argue everything to death and know the reasons for every action?
9. Does your child want to help because it will get the project done?
10. Does your child seem taken aback when you react emotionally when you are only having a discussion?

Descriptors 1-5 indicate Feeling. Descriptors 6-10 indicate Thinking. Mixed, no strong preference.

Judging or Perceiving?

1. Does your child need to close up a project or a conversation before being able to focus on something new?
2. Does your child need order and resent the breakdown of structure?
3. Is your child inflexible when time is involved?
4. Does your child find it necessary to know what is going on?
5. Is your child concerned with appearance and neatness and etiquette?
6. Does your child need to be able to amend a project or continue a conversation no matter how long it has gone on?
7. Does your child seem to thrive on last-minute chaos?

8. Is your child a master at improvising or doing things on the spur of the moment?

9. Is your child easy-going and resigned to "whatever happens, happens"?

10. Does your child seem late and sloppy and unfinished?

Descriptors 1-5 indicate Judging. Descriptors 6-10 indicate Thinking. Mixed, no strong preference.

ESTP
"The Ultimate Realists"
(10.5% of Americans)

Here is your football player as well as the boy who wants to take everything apart to see how it works. He will fall into religion because it's there, and go along because his family goes or his wife goes. Church appeals because it's traditional and gives him what he needs without interfering with the other parts of his life. This child rarely rebels against what he had grown up with until he is faced with an emergency that he has no compartment for. Give him structure and tradition, but make it logical and fun.

Many movies starring Clint Eastwood or Harrison Ford provide good role models for this child. He will be responsive to "maverick critic" roles in which the hero is outside of the system, but has justice on his side. Provide plenty of action, explosions, and effects and let him explore how to make his own life full of effects and excitement. You can also help him learn to relax and focus so he doesn't find himself off-center in a bad time.

ESTJ
"Life's Administrators"
(10.5% of Americans)

Here is the boy who will direct his family, his pets, his friends, and fall in love with anything that presents logic, order and tradition. He will surround himself with admirers and want to be quarterback rather than a lineman. If you do not appeal to his need for sense and sensibility, he will turn to the church as a way to get morality and agreement for a call to order in his life. Provide him with tradition, justice, and a high sense of purpose and reason so he will not fall back upon the church.

Give this child plenty of historical accounts of successful leaders, but also provide a smattering of role models who lead revolutions or bucked the system. Read him books about Ben Franklin as well as books about Thomas Jefferson. Help him build a Ptolemaic version of the solar system and then show him Copernicus. This will help him understand that the rules are important, but "the map is not the territory" in that rules need to change when our understanding of reality changes. Let him watch *The Right Stuff,* for the portrayal of John Glenn, and *A Man for All Seasons,* so that he can learn that rules can take over people's lives.

ESFP
"You Only Go Around the World Once in Life"
(10.5% of Americans)

This girl will need to party. She'll need a lot of friends and a lot to do. She will love social events, holidays, and any way to celebrate the traditions of life. She won't need a lot of structure, but she will need joy and celebration. She will turn to the church with shining eyes of excitement over the pageantry. Give this child the gift of celebration and the gift of a large crowd of supportive friends. She needs an Atheist community who have their own way of making life fun.

There are some wonderful, strong, and maverick role models emerging for girls. The recent movies, *Matrix* and *Elizabeth* are good movies for this reason. She will be under pressure to be fun instead of smart, so showing her a world where a woman can live an action-packed life without being stupid is a must. Movies about women athletes and explorers are also great. Get her into a group where there is plenty of activity such as a sport or a dance group. Join in with her.

Taking karate classes together or joining a folk dance club or even jogging together will go miles where talking about heady stuff will fall short.

ESFJ
"Hosts and Hostesses of the World"
(10.5% of Americans)

This girl will be the one who "mommies" everything. She will bandage up her dolls and hang on every word about helping out. She will want to direct everyone and help them find the right way to comfort and happiness. She is very vulnerable to religion for the appeal to her to organize the social events and direct her children into a better life. Give her something to organize and a mission in life with plenty of people to aid and teach. (This type is most grade-school teachers)

There are a couple of movies that are humorous examples of what can go wrong with trying to control people. Jane Austen's *Emma* is a charmer and subtle enough not to be preachy. *Cold Comfort Farm* is also delightful and will let your child see that she can overreach her bounds yet still land on her feet. She needs strong role models such as Elizabeth I or Marie Curie. Religion is part of tradition for this child, so offering Atheist tradition is a must. Let her explore the origins of etiquette and the reasons behind the reasons so that she can better understand that organization does not have to be control.

ENTP
"One Exciting Challenge After Another"
(5.75% of Americans)

This boy will turn your house upside down and inside out. You'll pull him off the chandeliers and scream when he rides a box down the stairs. He is a ball of motion and all of it in costume with a wild army of imaginary friends. He will tackle anyone and anything and ruthlessly destroy your entire life. Present yourself as authority to him and you'll be torn up faster than you can draw breath. He won't appreciate traditional religion, but he'll go for drugs, weird cults, far-out defying ideas and anything antiestablishment. Let this one go bungee-jumping so he won't bungee-jump his mind. Plenty of real thrills and challenges will keep him away from the fast life.

Show this maverick Carl Sagan or Richard Feyman. Let him watch *Mosquito Coast* or *Tucker* and encourage him to have patience. The world will appreciate his greatness by and by. This boy will have to fight and he'll fight you if you get in the way. The better solution is to point the way and stand aside. Help him with stories of men who learned that they had to be persistent and keep trying, over and over if need be. Enchant him with stories of Feynman, who played drums in his spare time away from physics. He'll be naturally drawn to video games; get him intrigued with inventing video games rather than wasting thousand of hours just being a spectator. Keep saying to yourself, "don't stand in his way." If you offer religion as an obstacle, he'll be perverse and join some cult to see for himself. Force him to go to some boring lecture on religion and he'll see for himself.

ENTJ
"Life's Natural Leaders"
(5.75% of Americans)

This boy will boss anyone and everyone who comes his way. He needs to be the inventor of new games and will lead everyone on that snipe hunt. He despises tradition, but needs authority and to be authority. He will found the new organization to eradicate religion, but he will also be vulnerable to lead new religions and to command in the upper levels of the Scientologists and the New Age cults. He needs to compete and to compete in a new way. Give him a real cause and he will become a doctor or a lawyer or the entrepreneur who will openly condemn religion.

Did I say doctors and lawyers? Let this child watch all those emergency shows, where the hero is at the operating table or in court or out in the streets saving people. This child needs role models who have changed the world. *The Right Stuff* is a good movie also for this child. Find movies or books where the hero must fight the system to save someone's life. Captain Picard of *Star Trek: the Next Generation* is a great role model. Stories of engineers and inventors are also a must. But this child needs to understand compassion and needs to know that it is up to him to show tolerance or he will be consumed by guilt at some mid-life crisis and a target for religion. Give him role models of older, wiser people and not just the ruthless surgeon who is brilliant and suppressed.

ENFP
"Giving Life an Extra Squeeze"
(5.75% of Americans)

This girl represents all the fairies and all the animal lovers of the world. She is so sympathetic that she will make you believe in ghosts. She loves everyone and everything and is terrified of death and hurt in others. She is the dancer and the lover and the adventurer, but she will be the one into drugs and the occult – in a big way. She will run to those faith healing frenzies and run away to California because some guru projects love. Make her life one that is filled with creative activity. Give this one the mice to make a "mouse world." Give and give and give, for she needs all the love and acceptance you have and more.

Jane Austen knew this character. *Sense and Sensibility* is a portrayal of an ENFP and an ISFJ. But the younger sister gets herself in trouble and understands that she went too far. Is is gentle caution without censuring the child. Lucid dreaming or movies about virtual reality such as *Matrix* are a way to teach this child that reality is often bound up in perception and that clearer perception comes with practice. Giving her a book on lucid dreaming may help her to understand that she can control her own mind to provide enough weird entertainment so that she does not have to seek it under more dangerous circumstances. This is another maverick type, so if you stand in the way, you will offer this child a reason to be perverse and do just the opposite of what you want. It is better to be sympathetic with people who find the world as it is to be BORING and point them in creative directions instead of pushing them into destructive directions.

ENFJ
"Smooth Talking Persuaders"
(5.75% of Americans)

This girl will make you think that children need to be locked up. She will convince everyone on the playground that Santa is a "real" guy. She is the church's darling because she has the bravery and the ability to go out there and sell. Boys of this type are the oil that grease the marketing industry. Creative, dedicated, and accomplished, it's hard to criticize these children. She will sell Scientology to anyone and everyone, even you. So give her the means and the reason to sell Atheism and everyone will fall to her charm and her grace.

A good movie for this child is *Wag the Dog,* a cautionary tale about the power of the media. This child will be a sucker or stick it to the suckers. The rare boy of this type will be so slick that he will be tempted to rule the universe with one hand out and the other in your wallet. Envision Jim Jones and the TV religious cults. The point of personality typing is not to pigeonhole, but to eliminate the prejudice and offer a way out that is in accordance with the child's preferred way of seeing the world. *Game Show* is a good movie for this child. This child needs to understand that there are consequences to lying and cheating, if only in the mind of the cheater. This child needs to see that the passion and conviction of honesty are far more winning than hypocrisy and charm to obtain short-term goals. Set the sights on the long term.

ISTP
"Ready to Try Anything Once"
(5.75% of Americans)

This child is quiet and has difficulty telling you what is wrong. His emotions are buried and he looks like nothing bothers him. But he is easily overlooked and invisible to everyone. He seems all right, but secretly he's in the bathroom shooting up on coke so he can deal with being social. This is Sherlock Holmes. Holmes was brilliant, but Holmes was extremely private about his coke addiction. You won't know that this child has joined the Catholics. This child needs a lot of science. Not a little to get him started, but a constant stream of names and forms and orders and phyla and traits and rules. Overlook his room, and watch him early to try to understand the life behind that closed face. Be swift and thorough to counteract a hint of a question. If you wait for him to actually talk about religion, he's already joined.

Thirty-two films about Glenn Gould is a must for this child and you to watch. And give him his own copy of the *Sherlock Holmes* videos. You should watch them as well. Understand that this child is clued into minutiae. Never lie. Never even white-lie. Be prepared for a deluge from time to time of ideas and information. The worst thing for this child is to tell him to shut up once he gets started. And don't turn away when he's absorbing. Remember Sherlock. Touch this child very gently when he is being open. Don't face him head on, but gently touch his shoulder and encourage him to talk or listen. If he is too old, it might freak him out, but he will remember it forever.

ISTJ
"Doing What Should be Done"
(5.75% of Americans)

This child is also quiet, but very, very, very, *very* intense. This child is the one who put his head through the window as a toddler just to show you that he was mad. He has

135

suppressed passions and an insatiable need for order and reason. He will work on projects long past the endurance of any other child and he will seem like a clock that is wound too tightly. This child is extremely vulnerable to traditional religions. Know, from the moment he enters the world that he will crave the order, the answers and the dedication of the church. He will need a reason for his stormy inner life and a mission to keep him going. He will be easily exhausted by school and despised on the playground. The church hunts down these children who are the backbone of the dedicated workers in the background of the pageantry. Love this difficult child and give him science and a lot of books on psychology. Give him a solitary sport for his intense passions and an endless supply of projects.

Spock – that is the final word for this child. Rent all the *Star Trek* videos. Some are corny, but watch what happens when Spock is trying to deal with a situation and McCoy attacks him for not being open or emotional. This child needs to see that he can maintain his cool but also reach out. Spock is a great example of a man who is private and dedicated, yet not a monk. Point out to your child that Spock has his traditions, which are very important to him, but that they do not affect his work. Give your child traditions for private support. Meditation, space, sacred time. Give him the effects of religion without the trappings.

ISFP
"Sees Much But Shares Little"
(5.75% of Americans)

This girl is the one that no one in school sees. She sits in the back of the class and quietly reads her books. She never volunteers in a discussion but stays after class to help the teacher clean the erasers. She is another pet lover and will secretly die if the pet dies. You can watch her face as the tears well up but no sound comes out of her. She will have one friend and will need a full and varied family life. She craves fun and love but will not seek it out. This child is a victim. She will give up all her toys and money to anyone who asks for it. She will buy friends and hang onto anyone who is kind once – even if they beat her to a pulp every day after that. Give this child security. Give her privacy and things to look after like a garden or a pet. Don't expect her to shine, but she will love you forever if you love her when she is young.

Let this girl watch *Persuasion*, another Jane Austen movie. Jane Austen is wonderful for girls because she is brilliant, critical, satirical, but not overtly religious. Church is only a part of the social culture in her books, unlike other novels such as *Little Women*, where it is a vital part of a moral message. The character of Anne is this personality type, wide-eyed and listening, but seldom asserting herself. The outcome of the story will give this girl courage. She needs to learn that if she does not speak up, she will be left behind – another needy person who will turn to religion for solace and a reason for her being good and receiving nothing for it.

ISFJ
"A High Sense of Duty"
(5.75% of Americans)

Here is "little Mary goodheart." Here is every nurse who just knew what you needed before you asked. Here is the one who will privately insist on working herself to death. She will pay no attention to her own health. She might be bossy and tyrannical in her own sphere, to the cats, or to her dolls, who happen to be patients in the hospital. This one needs to follow you around the house and do what you do. She will pick up after you and happily nurse you if you are sick. She needs religion in a big way because she needs to help the poor and the sick. Set her straight. Let her see that the church doesn't help. Then get her interested in helping the world in a way that is productive, rewarding and will not burn her out.

The church pins labels on people in order to make them aware and guilty for their traits, calling them "sins." This child's "sin" is that of pride. She needs role models to help

137

her separate doing good with reward in the afterlife. It is almost impossible for this personality type to be Atheistic, but duty to a god can be transformed into a performance for humanity. The only role models whom I can recommend are of the sort that trade service to the church for service to family such as the older sister in *Sense and Sensibility*. The key with this child is to constantly check to make sure that she is not taking on the burdens of the family assuming that it is her duty. Give her plenty of cartoons such as*"Bugs Bunny* to help her develop a sense of humor to moderate her serious dedication.

INTP
"A Love of Problem Solving"
(3% of Americans)

This one never went to church and never wanted to – UNLESS he decided to do an analysis of religion. Then he'll read every book there ever was on every cult, ghost, saint, and belief until you're so exhausted that you will scream at him to shut up. This boy is the brains of science. He ignores his emotions until they hit him on the head. He's so busy redesigning hyperspace that he'll forget to eat. And then he'll have the vision. No one else ever in the world has had a vision. He'll talk it to death and take his own pulse fifty times a day. This one was the baby everyone hated and the child at school with the thick glasses who knew all the answers and everyone hated him. He might not notice. Until it's too late. Then he may seek a private solace in drugs or the readings of the Sufi masters. Listen to this child as he rambles through life in ways you can't even fathom. Love this child early so he will come to you when he wakes up and his life is in shambles. He needs people, but he will never admit to his own sentimentality.

Give this child Science Fiction, but watch the growing movement in this genre to moralize and make characters believe in a "higher force." Sagan's movie *Contact* illustrates this point *ad nauseam*. Watch this movie with your child and stop the movie when Ellie cannot defend herself to the jury of people selecting the scientist to go into the machine. Talk then about why Ellie is afraid to stand up for the fact that she is an Atheist. This child will love characters like Data from *Star Trek, the Next Generation,* but Data's longing for something more must be explained as a way to grow and not some emptiness resulting from not having a god. With this child, you may have to spend some time going over things carefully to get him started on the right track or he will jump to his own conclusions and spend the rest of his life trying to prove that evolution is bogus.

INTJ
"Everything has Room for Improvement"
(3% of Americans)

You'd think this child had the secret to why everything doesn't work. He complains, loudly from the moment he is born until the day he dies. Nothing will satisfy him, nothing is good enough; and he can design everything over again to be better. Well, let him. You might be surprised. He's not complaining because he's ornery. He may really find the temperature too cold or too hot. He is sensitive but too much a grouch to admit it. This engineer is the last one to join a church. But this child should not be left on his own. He is vulnerable to drugs and the disasters of compartmentalizing his emotional life. He will fall in love hard. He will fall out of love hard. Make sure he gets a ton of security in the early years and then let him fix your stove and make your car run better and change all the lights in the house to fluorescents.

In the *Star Trek* series there is a host of great engineer role models. Almost no other series promotes characters who are in the story to make things work. All the engineers I know love these series because of Scotty, Geordi, and Miles O'Brien. Another wonderful role model for this child when he is older is Howard Roark of the *Fountainhead.* Many of Rand's characters are more intense than is ordinary, but they represent some of the few overtly Atheistic characters about.

This child may also suffer from a "duty" complex and need plenty of wry humor to protect himself from becoming a zealot. Humor will also protect him from giving into other religious people in the family for the sake of preserving peace and morality. Humor has to be amoral. You may find the next generation's humor offensive, and that is as it should be. *South Park* is one of the better shows to promote a healthy attitude of irreverence. Bugs Bunny, *Wayne's World, Monty Python, The Simpsons*, Groucho Marx, even Shakespeare all fill this function of poking fun at authority and morality. As an Atheist, your child needs this kind of humor, even if it means that you have to put up with being lampooned yourself. You've done your job if your child decides that he can one-up you. Keep telling yourself that impudence will save him from being brainwashed.

INFP
"Performing Noble Service to Aid Society"
(3% of Americans)

This girl will believe in the supernatural until she dies. She can *see* ghosts. If you dispute it she will burst into tears and secretly hate you forever. Yes, forever. She will never forget an attack. She is overly sensitive and vulnerable. She can feel the sky turn blue and hear trees tell her the secrets of life. Again, don't dispute it. She can. She is so finely tuned that most of what other people cannot see and hear is part of her waking life. Religion will tell her that this is okay, so you had better get on her side now. She'll look at you and instantly see all your problems and your flaws until you, too, will believe that she is a witch. Train her to use her talents and forgive her her bizarre ideas about life and she will show you a type of magic that can change the world – rather than spend her life reading deluded people's fortunes.

This child will find role models, needs role models, and will find a crusade, whether you have any input or not. Sarcasm can help this child where some rough humor will turn her away. Jane Austen is a master of subtle sarcasm and has a critical eye that will appeal to this child's sensitivity. Fairy tales provide a high level of morality without too much religion, with the exceptions of modern tales like those of Hans Christian Andersen. The approach with this kind of child is to offer plenty of religions so that she does not see good in only one, but sees good in everything and bad in everything. Then you can help explain to her that good and bad are human traits and religion is just a story.

INFJ
"An Inspiration to Others"
(3% of Americans)

This little girl was born an angel. Well maybe not. She was too sensitive to the cold and seemed too frail to live. She instantly invites protection. She is the little girl who dresses in fairy costumes but is so clean that she is heavenly. Mothers will rush up to crumple her gorgeous, shining self and then she will scream with terror. She is shy and she is fearful. She hates to be the center of attention but she will do all her work in school in original but neat precision. She is the one who turns to religion because it will set her free. It will bless her and let her shine and then sing her tired body to sleep. She seems already like a saint, transparent and expiring. Give this child silent strength. Hold her up so that she can touch the ceiling, but do not throw her or raise your voice. Show her the world of story telling and show how to make her life a fairy tale of color and love. Never criticize her, but show her how to get things done. She will be creative, efficient, and frail. She will expect death, so show her life and a purpose for living.

Again, this child needs a spread of information, spiced with some sarcasm. Self-critical to a fault, she will need constant monitoring from you that she is not taking on burdens that are not hers. She needs crusades like you need to breathe. Show her examples of real crusades such as the crusade for hygiene in hospitals. She will want to reinvent society, which is noble, but she will blame herself for falling short of her own standards. This child is very

141

vulnerable to "the poor in spirit," so she needs humor and warmth. Let her watch Julia Child or some of the other "how to" shows on television to turn her quest for perfection to a trade or an art. Heroes who are artists will appeal to this child as long as their struggle for perfection was met with artistic success.

Envoi

No matter how your child approaches the world, you must provide the spread of tools that will be needed to perceive it. Be accepting and loving. Instill confidence in your child's ability to choose the right tool for the right occasion. The world is full of injustice and unfairness. Don't tell your child otherwise. But show your child that it can also be full of joy, accomplishment, and the thrill of learning.

The real problem for Atheist parents is preventing the religion argument from becoming a focus of other problems. Too often, a child will rebel against a parent and reject values as well as family habits. A child of religious parents may often question those values if behavior in parents is contradictory and antagonistic, but Atheist parents are not immune by virtue of being more "rational." Often a bombastic Atheist parent can do more harm than good. The purpose of this book is to give an overview of personality and how conflicts relating to personality preferences can lead to a child being vulnerable to the call of religion.

The first rule might be to look upon a child with a positive light and not in a critical way. A child is not born broken with a need to be fixed. A child is not b orn errant with a need to be guided. Evidence supports the idea that children show strong preferences even from infancy, so a parent will be ahead of the game in working within those preferences instead of at cross purposes to them. If you, as a parent, can separate out mental style from the argument at hand, many arguments will dissipate and the real issues will emerge. This will enable your child to develop trust in your ability to guide and give advice.

Learn your own preferences. Do you see wrong when everyone else is trying to be fair? Do you shout that your feelings are hurt when the argument is over ideas and facts and goals? Do you feel that everyone around you is in fantasy land rather than dealing with reality? Do you feel that no one you know has any ability to get out of the rut and rote of method? Do you feel that everyone else is a control freak? Do you feel that you're the only person in your life with any appreciation for getting things done on time? Do you feel invaded by the world and want to be alone? Do you feel that there is not enough time in the day to appreciate the endless variety of life and resent the boredom of confinement?

Think of your children. If you feel put out, how do they feel? If you yell first, are you putting them on the defensive? Families get into ruts where personality determines a set fight that continues year after year. Think of your own parents. Do you fight with them over the same issues or in the same context year after year?

I have presented a loose guide to the Myers Briggs Test Indicator with a slant for children. Everyone is different; some children will be hard to understand, while others will be easily predictable. Remember that introverted children will show a "public personality" that may take on characteristics opposite to their true nature. Enjoy your children. Let them associate Atheism with fun and love and warmth. Why should the religious have the monoply on goodness? The world is a rough place, and you can start by trying to understand rather than aggravate. Even a child who does turn to religion may remember you with love and respect rather than with terror and anger.

Appendices

Recommended Movies

Planet of the Apes series. This series is B-grade but suited for younger audiences who can deal with Godzilla-type science fiction. They are a little dark, but beautifully portray religion as humorous and humanity as not at all noble. A good balance for those children who tend to be "better" than everyone else.

Jane Austen movies. While romantic almost to a flaw, Jane's portrayals of human quirks and light sarcasm are vital to a sensitive child. She is subtle but scathing, and the books are more sarcastic than the movies.

Clint Eastwood movies. Often dark, Clint likes to portray a loner figure who is cynical, but moral even though he is often pitted against a corrupt system. A good bet for those children who need explosions and car chases.

Escape from New York and *Escape from LA*. Snake Pliskin is another dark anti-hero who is cynical but moral in a way which is not religious, but ethical. His sense of justice wins over the hearts of many children who crave justice but cannot tolerate the moral pablum they are fed in school.

Bugs Bunny. Bugs is great for young children and older children. The wonderful thing about Bugs is that he has no anxiety. He is afraid when he needs to be, but carries no guilt or anxiety. He is irreverent and sarcastic. Nothing is sacred to Bugs, but he is always on the side of justice. Bugs is the leader of irreverent humor which is absolutely necessary when one is faced with dogma, brainwashing, moral idiocy, or the church. Imagine Bugs stuck in church, listening to some holy man, and you will have a great weapon to give your children. Humor is one of the few ways that your child can survive the playground politics of public school. If he or she is up on the latest "taboo" cartoon show, your child

145

will never suffer from being left out and ridiculed. Children are open to humor in ways beyond any church can control. "Bugs to start and Monty Python to finish" is one of my "rules."

James Bond. Great movies, a lot of action and no religion make these movies favorites of many generations. Many action movies are starting to get very heavy handed and raise all sorts of religious questions as well as affirming basic religious prejudice. *Air Force One* and *Contact* are movies that are of the worst of this type. Of older movies, *War of the Worlds* is one of Hollywood's greatest propaganda movies of a religious nature, disguised as Science Fiction.

Matrix and other "reality-check" movies are good in combination with studying lucid dreaming. This gives an "other worldly" child a real grip on what his mind can do to fool him. *Fairies* almost does this, but ends up not solving the question of whether or not there were fairies. Watch for covert mystical messages in these movies. Even Dr. LaBerge, who is a brilliant scientist, falls into mysticism from time to time. These are "edge" movies like the whole *Star Trek* series where the god issue is of the Transcendental school and can become part of the most logical person's framework. A child who is already skeptical has few problems with these movies and derives great benefit from them. Most Science Fiction tends to be agnostic or exploring the boundaries of religion. Fantasy also does this, but falls too much into mysticism. Many children will be into the other-world aspects of Fantasy and Science Fiction and find the morality satisfying, and this does not hurt them if they have a good grounding in skepticism and humor.

There are a host of great war movies, such as *Bridge over the River Quai,* which introduce a child to some great reasons for morality but also teach them that most people are sheep. *Apocalypse Now,* and *Great Escape* are examples of this genre. Be careful about showing these movies to sensitive children who might take them in a personal way and make it their mission to single-handedly change the world.

Another group of movies that show the destructive nature of religion are historical accounts. The new movie about Elizabeth I is dark and very accurate. *Beckett* is another movie where a man's life is destroyed by religion, although it is meant to be a depiction of a saint. *Stealing Heaven* is one of the most antireligious movies in the genre. It is a story about Abélard and Héloïse, a couple who were subtly persecuted by the church. *Aguirre the Wrath of God, Cabesa de Vaca,* and *The Mission* are very dark movies, good for teens about the horrors of the Catholic conquest of the Americas.

Recommended Books

Anything by Carl Sagan. His book *Demon-Haunted World* is a fabulous look at the UFO craze and knowledge in general. Sagan is full of awe and very devoid of religious mysticism.

Ayn Rand is heavy handed and can be easily lampooned, but is excellent for teenagers. She not only is overtly Atheistic, but shows people what worship of mediocrity can do. *We the Living* is her best book, but it is set in Russia and is very dark. *Anthem* is very short and a bit like Science Fiction, but it is a good introduction for a child who doesn't like to read.

Robert A. Heinlein is a Libertarian, but he also is an Atheist. His *Stranger in a Strange Land* can be taken in a mystical way, but it is full of subtle satire about religion.

H. P. Hogan is another satirical Atheistic Science Fiction author. Clark can be very mystical, but *2001* is good. Asimov is pretty clean; Herbert introduces a child to the politics of religion and is cynical.

Jane Austen is great for girls with a tendency toward romantic "boy meets girl" books. Many romance books fall into god-belief on a covert level. They encourage falling prey to the "happily ever after" syndrome which can lead to feeling broken and looking for a fix. For younger girls, Joan Aiken and mysteries can be an improvement on the romance novels.

Sherlock Holmes is great for all ages and leads a child into the mystery genre, which like the action and true-life adventure novels to be amoral. These novels are neutral, not offering reasons for being non-religious or religious, although some of the characters might be either way.

Suggested Reading for Parents

Baldwin, Rahima, *You are Your Child's First Teacher*. Berkeley, California: Celestial Arts, 1989.

Bettelheim, Bruno, *The Uses of Enchantment: The Meaning and Importance of Fairy Tales*. New York: Vintage Books, Random House, 1975.

Briggs, Dorothy Corkille, *Your Child's Self-Esteem: The Key to Life*. Garden City, NewYork: Doubleday and Company, Inc., 1975.

Gardner, Howard, *Frames of Mind: The Theory of Multiple Intelligences*. New York: Basic Books, HarperCollins Publishers, Inc., 1997.

Harary, Keith, Ph.D., and Donahue, Eileen, Ph.D., *Who Do You Think You Are? Explore Your Many-Sided Self with The Berkeley Personality Profile*. New York, Harper San Francisco, HarperCollins Publishers, Inc., 1994.

Hess, Karl, *Capitalism for Kids: Growing up to be Your Own Boss.*Wilmington, Delaware: Enterprise Publishing, Inc., 1987.

Kroeger, Otto and Thuesen, Janet M., *Type Talk: The 16 Personality Types that Determine How We Live, Love, and Work.* New York: Dell Trade, BantamD o u b l e d a y Dell Publishing Group, Inc., 1988.

Kuhn, Thomas S., *The Structure of Scientific Revolutions.* Chicago, The University of Chicago Press, 1962.

LaBerge, Stephen, Ph.D., *Lucid Dreaming.* New York: Ballantine Books, 1985.

Mendelsohn, Robert S., MD., *How to Raise a Healthy Child... In Spite Of Your Doctor.* New York: Ballantine Books, 1984.

Meyers, Isabel Briggs, *Gifts Differing: Understanding Personality Type.* New York: David Black Publishers, 1995.

Montagu, Ashley, *Touching: The Human Significance of Skin.* New York: Columbia University Press, 1971.

Sagan, Carl, Ph.D., *The Demon-Haunted World: Science as a Candle in the Dark.* New York: Random House, 1995.

Sears, William, M.D., *Parenting the Fussy Baby and the High Need Child: Everything you Need to Know.* Boston, Massachusetts: Little, Brown, and Company, 1996.

Shulman, Michael, *The Passionate Mind: Bringing up an Intelligent and Creative Child.* New York: The Free Press, MacMillan Inc., 1991.

Sowell, Thomas, *Late-Talking Children.* New York: Basic Books, HarperCollins Publishers, Inc., 1997.